JANE'S POCKET BOOK
MAJOR COMBAT AIRCRAFT

D. B. Gallagher USMC
510.64.4870

JANE'S POCKET BOOK
MAJOR COMBAT AIRCRAFT

NEW EDITION

Compiled by Michael J. H. Taylor and Kenneth Munson
Edited by John W. R. Taylor FRHistS, MRAeS, FSLAET

JANE'S

LONDON · SYDNEY

FIRST PUBLISHED 1973
THIRD IMPRESSION 1975
SECOND EDITION 1978
THIRD EDITION 1981

COPYRIGHT © John W. R. Taylor 1973, 1978, 1981

ISBN 0 7106 0121 2

This edition is not available for sale in the United States, its dependencies, the Philippine Islands or the Dominion of Canada.

Printed in England by Netherwood, Dalton and Co. Ltd., Huddersfield

PUBLISHED BY JANE'S PUBLISHING COMPANY LTD
238 CITY ROAD, LONDON EC1V 2PU

FOREWORD

We live in an age when the quality of almost anything, from a motor car to the chairman of a nationalised industry, is judged on the basis of what he, she or it costs. The huge twin-engined F-14 Tomcat is generally reckoned to be the world's most formidable fighter aircraft because it costs more than most of the others. Yet, a few days before this Foreword was written, a report from the Middle East told of an F-14 being destroyed by a tiny, mass-produced MiG-21. What the unfortunate pilot of the Tomcat had not known was that the armament of the MiG included a Magic air-to-air missile, newly bought from France.

It may be mere coincidence that the comment most appropriate to this incident came from a Frenchman, Voltaire, who wrote two centuries ago that "God is on the side not of the heavy batallions, but of the best shots". Such a suggestion is reassuring if we believe that freedom from major war depends on the maintenance of a balance of power between East and West, rather than on the unlikely ability, or wish, of national leaders to live together peaceably. If Voltaire were wrong, the size of the Warsaw Pact air forces listed in our companion Pocket Book of *Air Forces of the World,* allied to the quality of Soviet warplanes described in this third edition of *Major Combat Aircraft,* would offer little hope for the future.

In fact, the efficiency of a modern air force is influenced by a wide variety of factors other than sheer numbers. For example, the Soviet Union appears to build the very best aircraft that it is capable of producing; the West builds the best it thinks it can afford. As a result, the West sometimes could (and often should) build better aircraft, particularly in terms of the all-weather capability that is so essential in Europe. It also places far too little emphasis on the desirability of using common equipment throughout allied air forces, from complete aircraft to ammunition and spanners. The East, on the other hand, can only envy NATO superiority in terms of aircrew and groundcrew training, ground control of combat air forces, air-launched 'smart' weapons, and engine life between overhauls. That such differences exist, cancelling out advantages and disadvantages on the other side, provides one explanation for 35 years of freedom from global war on our turbulent planet.

Like its predecessors, this edition of *Major Combat Aircraft* covers every known type in service or in production throughout the world, except for one or two obsolescent designs such as the piston-engined Mustang of the second world war which still fly with smaller air forces, mainly in Latin America. Its standards of authenticity and accuracy are those which have made *Jane's All the World's Aircraft* the indispensible reference book for professional aviation people throughout the world.

Once again the emphasis is on the finest available photographs, reproduced as large and as clearly as possible, and accompanied by high-quality three-view line drawings. The information is that for which users of the Pocket Books have asked, without extraneous historical and structural details. Anyone who requires that much detail can find it in the million and a half words of each annual edition of *Jane's All the World's Aircraft.* Almost all the photographs which appeared in the second edition have been replaced; the text has been completely revised and updated. In particular, the first-line equipment of the Chinese air forces is covered fully for the first time, and information on the major Soviet types is more complete and reliable than ever before.

JWRT

5

Single-seat light tactical strike-reconnaissance fighter (G91R and G91Y), and tandem two-seat trainer (G91T)

Photo, Drawing and Data: G91Y

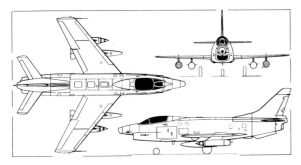

Power plant: Two General Electric J85-GE-13A turbojet engines (each 4 080 lb; 1 850 kg st with afterburning)
Wing span: 29 ft 6½ in (9.01 m)
Length overall: 38 ft 3½ in (11.67 m)
Max T-O weight: 19 180 lb (8 700 kg)

Max level speed: 600 knots (690 mph; 1 110 km/h) at S/L; Mach 0.95 at 30 000 ft (9 145 m)
Max rate of climb at S/L: with afterburning: 17 000 ft (5 180 m)/min
Service ceiling: 41 000 ft (12 500 m)
Typical combat radius at S/L: 323 nm (372 miles; 600 km)
Armament: Two 30 mm DEFA cannon and cameras in nose; four underwing attachment points for 1 000 lb bombs, 750 lb napalm tanks, 7 × 2 in rocket packs, 28 × 2 in rocket packs or 4 × 5 in rocket containers
Variants:
G91PAN: Modified pre-production aircraft; now used by aerobatic team of Italian Air Force
G91R/1/1A/1B: First production versions. Fiat/Bristol Siddeley Orpheus 803 turbojet engine (5 000 lb; 2 270 kg st). Avionics improved in later versions, and armament changed from four 0.50 in Colt-Browning machine-guns and two underwing pylons to four guns and four underwing pylons in 1B
G91R/3: Two 30 mm DEFA cannon instead of machine-guns
G91R/4: Four 0.50 in Colt-Browning machine-guns, four underwing pylons
G91T: Tandem two-seat trainer; two 0.50 in machine-guns, two underwing pylons
G91Y: Strike-reconnaissance version; see main description above
In service with: Air forces of Angola (G91R/4), German Federal Republic (G91R/3 and G91T/3), Italy (G91R/1/1A/1B, G91T/1 and G91Y), and Portugal (G91R/4)

Tandem two-seat basic and advanced trainer, single-seat operational trainer and light attack aircraft

Photo: AT-26 Xavante
Drawing and Data: MB 326GB

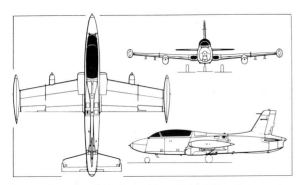

Power plant: One Rolls-Royce Viper 20 Mk 540 turbojet engine (3 410 lb; 1 547 kg st)
Wing span: over tip-tanks: 35 ft 7¼ in (10.854 m)
Length overall: 35 ft 0¼ in (10.673 m)
Max T-O weight: with full internal fuel, wingtip and underwing tanks, and 1,695 lb (769 kg) armament: 11 500 lb (5 216 kg)
Max level speed: trainer version: 468 knots (539 mph; 867 km/h)
Service ceiling: attack version: 39 000 ft (11 900 m)

Combat radius: attack version at max T-O weight with max fuel, 1 695 lb (769 kg) armament, fuel reserve, out at 20 000 ft (6 100 m), return at 25 000 ft (7 620 m): 350 nm (403 miles; 648 km)
Armament: Up to 4 000 lb (1 814 kg) of ordnance optional, on six underwing attachments. Weapon loads can include various arrangements of 2.75 in FFAR, Hispano-Suiza SURA 80 mm, 5 in HVAR, and Matra 122 rocket packs and rockets; 12.7 mm gun pods, 7.62 mm Minigun, and Matra SA-10 30 mm gun packs; 500 lb bombs; AS.12 missiles; and a reconnaissance pack

Variants:

MB 326: Two-seat basic trainer; Viper 11 engine
MB 326B/F/M: Two-seat trainer and light attack; Viper 11 engine
MB 326E: Two-seat advanced trainer for Italian AF; strengthened wings, six underwing hardpoints
MB 326GB/GC: Two-seat trainer/counter-insurgency versions, with airframe modifications; more powerful engine. Latter assembled by EMBRAER (Brazil) as *AT-26 Xavante*
MB 326H: Two-seat trainer; Viper 11 engine
MB 326K: Single-seat operational trainer/light ground attack; Viper 632-43 engine (4 000 lb; 1 814 kg st). *Impala Mk 2* based on this version but with Viper 540 engine. Two 30 mm DEFA cannon
MB 326L: Advanced trainer; 'K' airframe and two-seat cockpit
MB 339: Developed version: described separately

In service with: Argentine Navy (MB 326GB), air forces of Australia (MB 326H), Brazil *(AT-26 Xavante),* Dubai (MB 326K and L), Ghana (MB 326F and K), Italy (MB 326 and 326E), Paraguay *(AT-26 Xavante),* South Africa (MB 326M, known as *Impala Mk 1,* and *Impala Mk 2,* based on MB 326K), Togo *(AT-26 Xavante),* Tunisia (MB 326B, GB, K and L), Zaïre (MB 326GB and K), Zambia (MB 326GB) and Zimbabwe *(Impala)*

First flight 1980

Single-seat ground attack aircraft

Photo, Drawing and Data: MB 339 Veltro 2

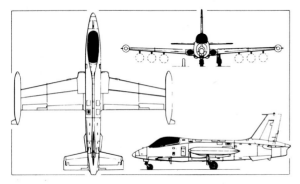

Power plant: One Rolls-Royce Viper Mk 632-43 turbojet engine (4 000 lb; 1 814 kg st)
Wing span: over standard tip-tanks: 35 ft 7½ in (10.858 m)
Length overall: 36 ft 0 in (10.972 m)
Max T-O weight: with external stores: 13 558 lb (6 150 kg)

Max level speed at S/L: 480 knots (553 mph; 889 km/h)
Max rate of climb at S/L: approx 6 560 ft (2 000 m)/min
Service ceiling: 44 500 ft (13 565 m)
Combat radius (hi-lo-hi): 455 nm (524 miles; 843 km)
Armament: Two 30 mm DEFA cannon (each with 125 rds) in lower forward fuselage. Up to 4 000 lb (1 814 kg) of external stores on four inner underwing hardpoints (each of 1 000 lb; 454 kg capacity) and two outer points (each 750 lb; 340 kg). Provisions on two innermost stations for two Macchi gun pods, each with either a 30 mm DEFA cannon and 120 rds or a 12.7 mm AN/M-3 machine-gun and 350 rds. Other typical loads can include two Matra 550 or Sidewinder air-to-air missiles (outer stations); four 1 000 lb or six 750 lb bombs; six SUU-11A/A 7.62 mm Minigun pods (1 500 rds/pod); six Matra 155 launchers, each for eighteen 68 mm rockets; six Matra F-2 practice launchers, each for six 68 mm rockets; six LAU-68/A or LAU-32/G launchers, each for seven 2.75 in rockets; six Aerea AL-25-50, AL-18-50 or AL-12-80 launchers, each respectively for twenty-five 50 mm, eighteen 50 mm or twelve 81 mm rockets; four LAU-10/A launchers, each with four 5 in Zuni rockets; six Aerea BRD bomb/rocket dispensers; six Aermacchi 11B29-003 bomb/flare dispensers; photographic pod with four 70 mm Vinten cameras; or two 71.5 Imp gallon (325 litre) drop-tanks
Variants:
MB 339A: Initial production tandem two-seat trainer version, first flown in 1976
MB 339K Veltro 2 (Greyhound): Single-seat version, optimised for ground attack; first flown 1980
In service with: M.B.339A with air forces of Italy (delivery of 100 under way) and Peru (on order)

First flight 1962

AÉROSPATIALE SUPER FRELON (France)

Heavy assault and anti-submarine helicopter

Photo, Drawing and Data: SA 321G Super Frelon

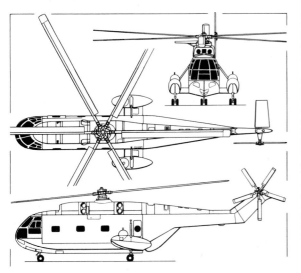

Power plant: Three Turboméca Turmo IIIC6 turboshaft engines (each 1 550 shp)
Main rotor diameter: 62 ft 0 in (18.90 m)
Length overall: 75 ft 6⅝ in (23.03 m), rotors turning
Max T-O weight: 28 660 lb (13 000 kg)
Cruising speed at S/L: 135 knots (155 mph; 250 km/h)
Max rate of climb at S/L: 1 312 ft (400 m)/min
Service ceiling: 10 325 ft (3 150 m)
Range at S/L: 442 nm (509 miles; 820 km)
Endurance: in ASW role: 4 h
Armament: Four homing torpedoes or two Exocet air-to-surface missiles
Variants:
SA 321F: 34/37-passenger commercial airliner version
SA 321G: Anti-submarine version. Central navigation system, Doppler radar and radio altimeter; Sylphe panoramic radar with IFF capability and dipping sonar; ORB 31D or ORB 32 Héraclès target designation radar for use with Exocet installation
SA 321H: Version for air force and army service, without stabilising floats or external fairings on each side of lower fuselage. Turmo IIIE6 engines. No de-icing equipment
SA 321Ja: Utility and public transport version, to carry 27 passengers or cargo (external load of up to 11 023 lb; 5 000 kg, or internal load of 8 818 lb; 4 000 kg)
In service with: Air forces of China, France (Air Force, Navy), Iraq, Israel, Libya, Malta, Pakistan, South Africa and Zaire

First flight 1965

Assault helicopter

Photo and Drawing: SA 330E Puma HC Mk 1
Data: SA 330L Puma

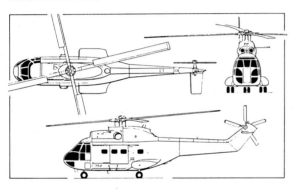

Power plant: Two Turboméca Turmo IVC turboshaft engines (each 1 575 shp)
Main rotor diameter: 49 ft 2½ in (15.00 m)
Length overall: 59 ft 6½ in (18.15 m)
Max T-O weight: 16 315 lb (7 400 kg)

Max cruising speed at S/L: 139 knots (160 mph; 258 km/h)
Max rate of climb at S/L: 1 200 ft (366 m)/min
Service ceiling: 15 750 ft (4 800 m)
Max range at normal cruising speed, no reserves: 297 nm (341 miles; 550 km)
Armament: Wide range of armament can be carried, including side-firing 20 mm cannon, axial-firing 7.62 mm machine-guns, rockets and missiles
Variants:
SA 330B: Powered by Turmo IIIC4 engines (each 1 328 shp). Version for French forces
SA 330C/H: Military export versions, initially with Turmo IVB engines (each 1 400 shp). No air intake anti-icing. From end of 1973 H versions delivered with Turmo IVC engines (each 1 575 shp) and intake anti-icing
SA 330E: Royal Air Force version, designated *Puma HC Mk 1*
SA 330F/G: Civil passenger and cargo versions, initially with Turmo IVA engines (each 1 435 shp) and later with Turmo IVC engines
SA 330J/L: Civil (J) and military (L) versions introduced in 1976: main rotor blades of composite materials, and increased max T-O weight
In service with: Air forces of Abu Dhabi, Algeria, Argentina, Belgium, Brazil, Chad, Chile, Ecuador, Ethiopia, France (Air Force, Army), Gabon, Indonesia, Iraq, Ivory Coast, Kenya, Kuwait, Lebanon, Malawi, Mexico, Nepal, Nigeria, Pakistan, Philippines, Portugal, Qatar, Romania, Senegal, South Africa, Spain, Sudan, Togo, Tunisia, UK and Zaïre

Single-seat supersonic fighter (Mks 3, 6, 52 and 53) and two-seat operational trainer (Mks 4, 5, 54 and 55)

Photo: Lightning F Mk 3
Drawing: Lightning F Mk 6
Data: Lightning F Mk 53

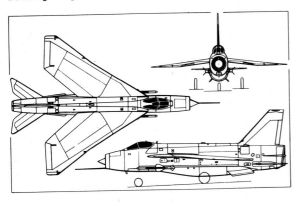

Power plant: Two Rolls-Royce Avon 302-C turbojet engines (each 16 300 lb; 7 393 kg st with afterburning)

Wing span: 34 ft 10 in (10.61 m)
Length overall: 55 ft 3 in (16.84 m), incl probe
Max T-O weight: approx 48 000 lb (21 770 kg)
Max level speed at operational height: above Mach 2 (1 146 knots; 1 320 mph; 2 124 km/h)
Armament: Two 30 mm Aden guns can be carried. Weapon bay can accommodate one of a variety of operational packs. These include a twin-Firestreak or twin-Red Top air-to-air missile pack, or a rocket pack with two retractable launchers for a total of 44 × 2 in spin-stabilised rockets. Two pylons beneath outer wings, each capable of carrying two 1 000 lb HE, retarded or fire bombs, two Matra 155 launchers for 18 SNEB 68 mm rockets apiece, two flare pods or two machine-gun pods
Current variants:
F Mk 3/3A. Rolls-Royce Avon 301, air-to-air missile armament only, and larger tail fin than original Mk 1, with square top. Reduced outer-wing sweep on F Mk 3A. Most converted later to F Mk 6
T Mk 4: Side-by-side two-seat unarmed trainer based on F Mk 1. Avon 201 engines and round-topped fin
T Mk 5: Side-by-side two-seat trainer based on Mk 3; Avon 301 engines, square-topped fin, provision for missiles
F Mk 6: Last production version for RAF; Avon 301s of 16 360 lb (7 420 kg) st each
F Mk 52: F Mk 2s transferred to Saudi Arabia
F Mk 53: Version for multi-role duties
T Mk 54: T Mk 4s transferred to Saudi Arabia
T Mk 55: Two-seat trainer
In service with: Air forces of Saudi Arabia (F Mk 52, F Mk 53, T Mk 54 and T Mk 55), and UK (F Mk 3, T Mk 4, T Mk 5 and F Mk 6)

Single-seat V/STOL strike/reconnaissance aircraft (GR Mk 3 and AV-8A) and two-seat operational trainer (T Mks 4, 4RN, 60 and TAV-8A)

Photo, Drawing and Data: Harrier GR Mk 3

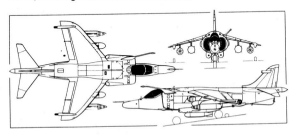

Power plant: One Rolls-Royce Pegasus Mk 103 vectored-thrust turbofan (21 500 lb; 9 752 kg st)

Wing span: combat: 25 ft 3 in (7.70 m); ferry: 29 ft 8 in (9.04 m)

Length overall: 45 ft 7.8 in (13.91 m) with laser nose

Max T-O weight: over 25 000 lb (11 340 kg)

Max speed at low altitude: over 640 knots (737 mph; 1 186 km/h) EAS

Max Mach number (in a dive): 1.3

Ceiling: over 50 000 ft (15 240 m)

Range with one in-flight refuelling: over 3 000 nm (3 455 miles; 5 560 km)

Armament: One underfuselage and four underwing pylons, all with ML ejector release units. Fuselage and inboard wing points stressed for up to 2 000 lb (910 kg) each, outboard underwing pair for up to 650 lb (295 kg) each; two strake fairings under fuselage can each be replaced by a 30 mm Aden gun pod and ammunition. The Harrier is cleared for operations with a maximum external load exceeding 5 000 lb (2 270 kg), and has flown with a weapon load of 8 000 lb (3 630 kg). It can carry 30 mm guns, bombs, rockets and flares of UK and US designs, and in addition to its fixed reconnaissance camera (in nose) can carry a five-camera reconnaissance pod.

Current variants:

GR Mk 3: Single-seat version with Pegasus 103 engine. Formerly GR Mk 1A (Pegasus 102) and originally GR Mk 1 (Pegasus 101)

T Mk 4: Two-seat version with Pegasus 103 engine. Formerly designated T Mk 2A with Pegasus 102 and originally T Mk 2 with Pegasus 101

T Mk 4RN: Royal Navy version to provide training for Sea Harrier

T Mk 60: Indian Navy equivalent of T Mk 6

AV-8A: Similar to GR Mk 3 but with provision for Sidewinder missiles. Known as *AV-8S Matador* in Spanish Navy

TAV-8A: Similar to T Mk 4; known as *TAV-8S* in Spanish Navy

AV-8C: Interim USMC update of AV-8A with extended-life airframe, forward-looking passive warning radar, tail warning radar, flare/chaff dispenser, lift improvement devices under fuselage, and secure voice system. All existing AV-8As to undergo modification

Big Wing Harrier: Advanced version proposed by BAe, with super-critical wing of greater span, thickness and area, capable of retrofit to existing Harrier GR Mk 3 or T Mk 4 fuselage; six underwing stores points; leading-edge wing-root extensions and cushion augmentation devices

In service with: Air forces of India (Navy, T Mk 60), Spain (Navy, AV-8S Matador and TAV-8S), UK (RAF, GR Mk 3 and T Mk 4; Royal Navy, T Mk 4RN) and USA (Marine Corps, AV-8A, AV-8C, TAV-8A)

BAe SEA HARRIER and McDONNELL DOUGLAS AV-8B ADVANCED HARRIER (UK/USA)

Single-seat V/STOL fighter, reconnaissance and strike aircraft
Photo: Sea Harrier FRS Mk 1
Drawing: AV-8B Advanced Harrier
Data: (A) Sea Harrier FRS Mk 1; (B) YAV-8B

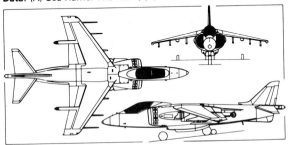

Power plant: (A) One Rolls-Royce Pegasus Mk 104 vectored-thrust turbofan engine (21 500 lb; 9 752 kg st); (B) same engine (US designation F402-RR-404), with new intakes and increased fuel
Wing span: (A) 25 ft 3¼ in (7.70 m); (B) approx 30 ft 4 in (9.25 m)
Length overall: (A) 47 ft 7 in (14.50 m); (B) 46 ft 4 in (14.12 m)
Max T-O weight: (A) approx 25 000 lb (11 340 kg); (B) 29 750 lb (13 494 kg)
Max level speed: (A) over 640 knots (736 mph; 1 185 km/h)
Strike radius: (A) 250 nm (288 miles; 463 km); (B, short take-off, with 7 Mk 82 Snakeye bombs and external fuel tanks, no loiter) more than 650 nm (748 miles; 1 204 km)
High altitude intercept radius: (A, with 3 min combat and reserves for vertical landing) 400 nm (460 miles; 750 km)
Armament: (A) As Harrier GR Mk 3 (which see), except for addition of Sidewinder installation similar to that of AV-8A, and provision for two air-to-surface missiles of Martel or Harpoon type
(B) Twin underfuselage gun/ammunition packs, each mounting a 25 mm US or 30 mm Aden cannon. Single 1 000 lb (454 kg) stores point on centreline, between gun packs. Three stores stations under each wing, of which inner pair on each side can carry auxiliary fuel tanks. Max external load is approx 7 000 lb (3 175 kg) for vertical T-O, nearly 17 000 lb (7 710 kg) for short T-O. Typical weapons include Mk 82 Snakeye bombs, and laser or electro-optically guided weapons. Angle Rate Bombing System, comprising a dual-mode (TV and laser) target seeker linked to HUD via digital computer; passive ECM

Variants:
Sea Harrier FRS Mk 1: British-designed maritime development of Harrier with raised cockpit, Ferranti Blue Fox multi-mode radar in redesigned folding nose, ECM in fin pod, underwing Sidewinder missiles, and revised operational avionics
Sea Harrier FRS Mk 51: Version of FRS Mk 1 for Indian Navy
YAV-8B: Prototypes (two converted AV-8As) for AV-8B; being followed by four full-scale development aircraft, first of which due to fly in late 1981. Longer-span supercritical wing, largely of composite materials, underfuselage lift-augmenting surfaces, larger wing flaps, drooped ailerons, redesigned air intakes, and increased external stores-carrying capability
AV-8B: Advanced version required by US Marine Corps, which plans for 336 from mid-1980s; awaiting production go-ahead
In service with: Indian Navy (Sea Harrier FRS Mk 51) and Royal Navy (Sea Harrier FRS Mk 1); AV-8B under development for USMC

Tandem two-seat basic and advanced trainer, with combat capability

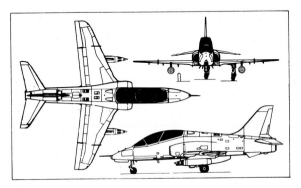

Power plant: One Rolls-Royce Turboméca RT.172-06-11 Adour Mk 151 non-afterburning turbofan engine (5 200 lb; 2 358 kg st)

Wing span: 30 ft 9¾ in (9.39 m)
Length overall: excluding probe: 36 ft 7¾ in (11.17 m)
Max T-O weight: 17 085 lb (7 750 kg)
Max level speed: 560 knots (645 mph; 1 038 km/h)
Max Mach number in dive: 1.2
Time to 30 000 ft (9 145 m): 6 min 6 s
Service ceiling: 50 000 ft (15 240 m)
Combat radius with 5 600 lb (2 540 kg) weapon load: 300 nm (345 miles; 556 km)
Ferry range with two 100 Imp gallon (455 litre) drop-tanks: 1 669 nm (1 922 miles; 3 093 km)
Armament: Provision for total external stores load of 5 660 lb (2,567 kg). Underfuselage centreline-mounted 30 mm Aden gun and ammunition pack. Two inboard underwing points, each capable of carrying a 1 000 lb (454 kg) stores load, including a Matra 155 launcher for eighteen 2.75 in air-to-ground rockets, or a cluster of four practice bombs. Provision for two outboard underwing pylons and a pylon in place of the ventral gun pack, each capable of carrying a 1 000 lb (454 kg) load. Some RAF Hawks will be modified to carry two AIM-9L Sidewinder air-to-air missiles for operational use in an emergency
In service with: Air forces of Finland (Mk 51), Indonesia (Mk 53), Kenya (Mk 52) and UK (T Mk 1)

Long-range anti-submarine and maritime reconnaissance aircraft

Photo: Nimrod MR Mk 2
Drawing and Data: Nimrod MR Mk 1

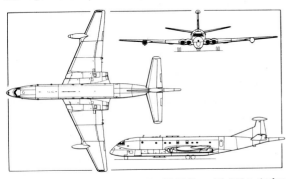

Power plant: Four Rolls-Royce RB 168-20 Spey Mk 250 turbofan engines (each 12 140 lb; 5 506 kg st)
Wing span: 114 ft 10 in (35.00 m)
Length overall: 126 ft 9 in (38.63 m)
Normal max T-O weight: 177 500 lb (80 510 kg)
Max speed for operational necessity, ISA+20°C: 500 knots (575 mph; 926 km/h)

Typical low-level patrol speed on two engines: 200 knots (230 mph; 370 km/h)
Max operating altitude: 42 000 ft (12 800 m)
Typical ferry range: 4 500-5 000 nm (5 180-5 755 miles; 8 340-9 265 km)
Armament and equipment: Bay in rear pressurised part of fuselage for active and passive sonobuoys. Ventral weapons bay can accommodate up to six lateral rows of ASW weapons, including up to nine torpedoes as well as bombs; up to six auxiliary fuel tanks; or a combination of fuel tanks and weapons. Pylon beneath each wing at approx one-third span, on which gun pods, rocket pods or mines can be carried. ASW equipment includes Sonics 1 C sonar and a new long-range sonar system. ASV 21 air-to-surface-vessel detection radar, Autolycus ionisation detector, and ECM gear. MAD (magnetic anomaly detector) in extended tail 'sting'. Searchlight in starboard external wing fuel tank
Variants:
MR Mk 1: Major current version, as described
R Mk 1: Similar to MR 1 but without MAD tailboom and with modified port-wing pod, for special reconnaissance
MR Mk 2: Updated standard to which 32 of RAF's MR Mk 1s are being converted; redelivery began in 1979. Advanced EMI Searchwater search radar, with greater range and sensitivity, Marconi AQS 901 acoustic processing and display system, armament which includes Stingray homing torpedoes, EWSM (early warning support measures) in wingtip pods, and other improved avionics
AEW Mk 3: Airborne early warning version, described separately
In service with: Royal Air Force (MR Mk 1, R Mk 1 and MR Mk 2)

Airborne early warning aircraft

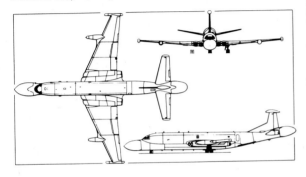

Power plant: Four Rolls-Royce RB 168-20 Spey Mk 250 turbofan engines (each 12 140 lb; 5 506 kg st)
Wing span: 115 ft 1 in (35.08 m)
Length overall: 137 ft 8½ in (41.97 m)

Max T-O weight: not released
Performance: not released, but assumed to be generally similar to that of Nimrod MR Mks 1 and 2 (which see). Fleet size of 11 aircraft is based on requirement for two aircraft to be on station for 24 hours of every day, one at 261 nm (300 miles; 483 km) and the other at 608 nm (700 miles; 1 127 km) from base. Aircraft systems are designed to detect low-flying aircraft at ranges of up to 261 nm (300 miles; 483 km)
Accommodation: Normal crew of ten, comprising a flight crew of four plus six systems/equipment operators in tactical compartment
Avionics and operational equipment: Three basic sensors to detect and classify targets: a Marconi multi-mode pulse-Doppler radar with identical antennae in nose and tail radomes; a passive radio/radar detection system; and an IFF system (which shares the same antennae as the radar) to identify friendly targets. Radar scanners, with very low sidelobe levels, each sweep through 180° in azimuth, and phased switching provides a full 360° coverage. Loral EWSM (electronic warfare support measures) are housed in the two wingtip pods. IFF system includes Cossor Jubilee Guardsman interrogator. ESM in pod on top of tail fin. Other equipment includes data link system, air data computer, dual INS, Tacan, and secure voice communications
In production for: Royal Air Force (deliveries due to begin in 1982)

Side-by-side two-seat light strike aircraft (Strikemaster, and Jet Provost Mks 51 and 52) and training aircraft (Strikemaster Mk 55 and Jet Provost Mks 3, 4 and 5)

Photo: Strikemaster Mk 80
Drawing and Data: Strikemaster

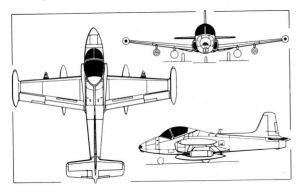

Power plant: One Rolls-Royce Viper Mk 535 turbojet engine (3 410 lb; 1 547 kg st)
Wing span: 36 ft 10 in (11.23 m) over tip-tanks
Length overall: 33 ft 8½ in (10.27 m)

Max T-O weight: 11 500 lb (5 215 kg)
Max level speed with 50% fuel, clean: at S/L: 391 knots (450 mph; 724 km/h); at 20 000 ft (6 100 m): 410 knots (472 mph; 760 km/h)
Rate of climb at S/L (training, internal fuel): 5 250 ft (1 600 m)/min
Range with 200 lb (91 kg) fuel reserve: at 8 355 lb (3 789 kg) AUW (training): 629 nm (725 miles; 1 166 km); at 10 500 lb (4 558 kg) AUW (combat): 1 075 nm (1 238 miles; 1 992 km); at max T-O weight: 1 200 nm (1 382 miles; 2 224 km)
Armaments and operational equipment: One 7.62 mm FN machine-gun, with 550 rds, in lower lip of each engine air intake. Four underwing hardpoints for up to 3 000 lb (1 360 kg) of external stores, or up to 2 650 lb (1 200 kg) with full fuel load. Weapon loads can include various arrangements of Matra launchers with 68 mm SNEB rockets, 540 LAU 68 rocket launchers, SURA 80 mm rockets, 2.75 in or 3 in rockets, napalm tanks, 540 lb ballistic or retarded bombs, 250 or 500 kg bombs, 65 or 125 kg bombs, practice bombs, 7.62 mm or 20 mm gun packs, BAe/Vinten five-camera reconnaissance pod, drop-tanks and gun camera
Variants:
Strikemaster: Mks 80-89 for air forces as listed; all similar externally
Jet Provost: Armed or unarmed trainer/light attack, all externally similar. More bulbous nose, different cockpit canopy, lower-rated Viper 202 engine (2 500 lb; 1 134 kg st) with shorter tailpipe
In service with:
Strikemaster: Air forces of Ecuador (Mk 89), Kenya (Mk 87), Kuwait (Mk 83), New Zealand (Mk 88), Oman (Mk 82 and Mk 82A), Saudi Arabia (Mk 80 and Mk 80A), Singapore (Mk 84) and Sudan (Mk 55)
Jet Provost: Air forces of Sri Lanka (T Mk 51), Sudan (T Mk 51 and T Mk 52) and UK (T Mk 3, T Mk 4 and T Mk 5)

Tandem two-seat single- or twin-engined armed helicopter

Photo and Data: AH-1S HueyCobra
Drawing: AH-1T SeaCobra

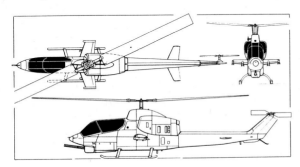

Power plant: One 1 800 shp Avco Lycoming T53-L-703 turboshaft engine
Main rotor diameter: 44 ft 0 in (13.41 m)
Length overall: 52 ft 11½ in (16.14 m), main rotor fore and aft
Max T-O weight: 10 000 lb (4 535 kg)
Max level speed: 123 knots (141 mph; 227 km/h) with TOW
Max rate of climb at S/L: 1 620 ft (494 m)/min
Service ceiling: 12 200 ft (3 720 m)
Max range at S/L: max fuel, reserves: 274 nm (315 miles; 507 km)

Armament: All AH-1S armed with M65 system (eight TOW anti-armour missiles on outboard underwing stations). Up-gun and Modernised AH-1S have new GE universal turret under nose, equipped initially with M197 three-barrel 20 mm Vulcan cannon (750 rds); 30 mm Hughes XM230E1 chain gun due for installation from mid-1981. These two versions also have Baldwin XM138 system enabling any one of five types of 2.75 in underwing rocket (mounted in launchers each containing from 7 to 19 tubes, and additional to the TOW capability) to be fired singly or in groups. Aircraft to full Modernised standard also have Kaiser HUD for pilot, Teledyne Systems digital fire control computer for turreted weapon and underwing rockets, Hughes laser rangefinder, AN/AAS-32 laser tracker, ECM, and infra-red signature suppression.

Variants:
AH-1G: Initial US Army production version with 1 400 shp T53-L-13 engine (derated to 1 100 shp); 93 converted to AH-1Q; these and 197 others uprated subsequently to Mod AH-1S
JAH-1G: Testbed version; used for trials with Hellfire laser-guided missile and GE M197 turret weapons
TH-1G. Dual-control trainer version of AH-1G
AH-1J SeaCobra: Pratt & Whitney (Canada) T400-CP-400 coupled turboshaft (1 250 shp for T-O), improved armament and Marine avionics. Built for USMC (69) and Iran (202 with TOW capability)
AH-1Q: Anti-armour version of AH-1G, with TOW missiles; 93 converted from AH-1G; subsequently upgraded to Mod AH-1S
AH-1R: T53-L-703 engine (1 800 shp); no TOW capability
Mod AH-1S: TOW-capable version for US Army; 290 produced by conversion of AH-1G/Q

(cont on page 33)

Bell Model 206L TexasRanger

First flight 1980

BELL MODEL 206L TEXASRANGER (USA)

Light multi-mission helicopter

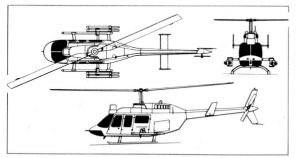

Power plant: One 500 shp Allison 250-C28B turboshaft engine in prototype; one 650 shp Allison 250-C30P specified for production aircraft

Main rotor diameter: 37 ft 0 in (11.28 m)
Length overall: 42 ft 4¾ in (12.92 m) with rotors turning
Max T-O weight: 4 150 lb (1 882 kg) with internal load; 4 250 lb (1 928 kg) with external jettisonable load
Max cruising speed, armed: 105 knots (121 mph; 195 km/h)
Max rate of climb at S/L, armed: 1 280 ft (390 m)/min
Max range, armed: 275 nm (317 miles; 510 km)
Accommodation: Pilot and weapons operator on side-by-side armoured seats for armed missions. Pilot and up to six passengers for personnel transport duties. Other mission roles include armed reconnaissance and surveillance, search and rescue, medical evacuation, command control and battlefield resupply
Armament: Can include four TOW missiles in two twin launchers, plus four reload missiles; or two seven-round pods of 2.75 in rockets; or two pods each containing two FN 7.62 mm machine-guns with 500 rds per gun; or four air-to-air missiles. Roof-mounted sight for TOW missiles has provisions for future installation of a forward-looking infra-red (FLIR) receiver and laser range-finder/designator
Development status: Prototype only in early 1981

Bell AH-1 Hueycobra *(cont from page 31)*

Production AH-1S: Initial production TOW version (100 built): new flat-plate canopy, improved avionics and instrumentation and (from c/n 67) composite rotor blades. Deliveries began August 1977
Up-gun AH-1S. Next 98 production S models, adding new universal 20/30 mm turret and increased electrical power
Modernised AH-1S. Fully-upgraded S version (see 'Armament' above). Deliveries of 99 production aircraft began November 1979.

US Army plans to bring all AH-1S variants up to this standard by mid-1980s, and also to convert 425 AH-1Gs to same standard
AH-1T Improved SeaCobra: Uprated AH-1J. T400-WV-402 coupled turboshaft (2 050 shp), longer fuselage, dynamic system of Bell 214; 57 ordered, incl 23 with TOW capability
In service with: Iran (AH-1J), Israel (AH-1G/S), Japan (AH-1S), Spain (Navy AH-1G) and USA (Army AH-1G/S HueyCobra, Marine Corps AH-1G HueyCobra and AH-1J/T SeaCobra)

First flight about 1960

BERIEV M-12 (Be-12) (USSR)

NATO Reporting Name *Mail*
Maritime reconnaissance amphibian; crew of three or four

Power plant: Two Ivchenko AI-20D turboprop engines (each 4 000 shp)
Wing span: 97 ft 5¾ in (29.71 m)
Length overall: 99 ft 0 in (30.17 m)
Max T-O weight: 64 925 lb (29 450 kg)
Max level speed: 328 knots (378 mph; 608 km/h)
Normal operating speed: 172 knots (199 mph; 320 km/h)
Rate of climb at S/L: 2 990 ft (912 m)/min
Service ceiling: 37 000 ft (11 280 m)
Max range: 2 158 nm (2 485 miles; 4 000 km)
Armament: Internal bomb bay. Provision for one large and one small external stores pylon under each outer wing panel
In service with: Soviet Navy

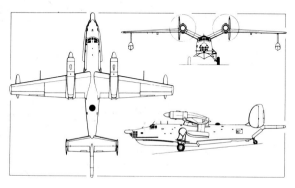

First flight 1952

Long-range strategic heavy bomber

Photo: B-52G Stratofortress
Drawing and Data: B-52H Stratofortress

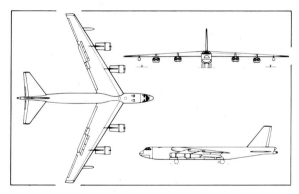

Power plant: Eight Pratt & Whitney TF33-P-3 turbofan engines (each 17 000 lb; 7 718 kg st)
Wing span: 185 ft 0 in (56.39 m)
Length overall: 160 ft 10.9 in (49.05 m)
Max T-O weight: more than 488 000 lb (221 350 kg)
Max level speed: at high altitude: 516 knots (595 mph; 957 km/h)

Cruising speed: at high altitude: 442 knots (509 mph; 819 km/h)
Service ceiling: 55 000 ft (16 765 m)
Max range: without in-flight refuelling: more than 8 685 nm (10 000 miles; 16 093 km)
Armament: One M61 Vulcan multi-barrel 20 mm gun in General Electric remotely controlled rear turret (four 0.50 in machine-guns in B-52G). Up to 20 Boeing AGM-69 SRAMs (short-range attack missiles): eight on rotary launcher in internal weapons bay and six under each wing; plus nuclear free-fall bombs
Variants in service:
B-52D: Pratt & Whitney J57-P-19W/J57-P-29W engines (each 10 000 lb; 4 535 kg st). Increased fuel tankage over earlier B-52A/B/C. Four 0.50 in machine-guns in manned tail turret
B-52G. Main variant. J57-P-43WB engines (each 13 750 lb; 6 237 kg st). 'Wet' wing with increased fuel capacity in integral tanks. Remotely controlled rear gun turret. Shorter vertical tail surfaces
B-52H: Improved power plant and defensive armament; otherwise generally as B-52G. Some 270 B-52G and H equipped with AN/ASQ-151 Electro-optical Viewing System (EVS) to improve low-level flight capability; further planned updates include Motorola ALQ-122 SNOE (Smart Noise Operation Equipment) countermeasures and Northrop AN/ALQ-155(V) advanced ECM; AFSATCOM kit for worldwide communications via satellite; ALR-46 digital radar warning receiver, ALQ-153 tail warning radar, and ITT Avionics ALQ-172 noise/deception jammers. Navigation and weapons delivery systems of G and H also to be upgraded (digital instead of analogue, and incorporating terrain comparison guidance)
In service with: US Air Force (316 B-52D/G/H operational in 1980; supported by small numbers of training, backup and test aircraft)

First flight (EC-137D) 1972

Airborne warning and control system (AWACS) aircraft

Photo, Drawing and Data: E-3A Sentry

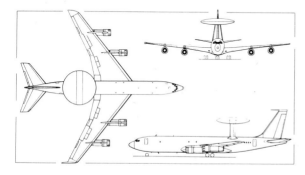

Power plant: Four Pratt & Whitney TF33-PW-100/100A turbofan engines (each 21 000 lb; 9 525 kg st)
Wing span: 145 ft 9 in (44.42 m)
Length overall: 152 ft 11 in (46.61 m)
Max T-O weight: 325 000 lb (147 400 kg)

Max level speed: 460 knots (530 mph; 853 km/h)
Service ceiling: above 29 000 ft (8 850 m)
Endurance on station: at 870 nm (1 000 miles; 1 610 km) from base, without in-flight refuelling: 6 h
Accommodation: Flight crew of four, plus 13 systems operators; latter number can vary according to mission
Operational equipment: Includes Westinghouse AN/APY-1 S-band surveillance radar, IFF, TADIL-C fighter control data link, IBM CC-1 or CC-2 central computer, twin Delco AN/ASN-119 Carousel IV inertial navigation sets, Northrop AN/ARN-120 Omega nav, Teledyne Ryan AN/APN-213 Doppler velocity sensor, data processing equipment. See under 'Variants' below for additional items in US/NATO standard E-3A
Variants:
EC-137D. Prototypes (two), converted from commercial Boeing 707-320B, for flight test and trials with competitive radars. Later brought up to E-3A standard
E-3A. Initial production version: 30 ordered by US Air Force by 1981, of 34 planned; deliveries began March 1977. First 23 of these are to 'core' configuration; from 24th USAF aircraft all E-3As (including 18 ordered by NATO for delivery from 1982) are to enhanced standard with added maritime surveillance capability, improved JTIDS communications system, larger-memory computer, improved data processing, and underwing provision for SDS (self-defence stores)
In service with: US Air Force; ordered for NATO

Advanced airborne command post (AABNCP)

Photo and Data: E-4B
Drawing: E-4A

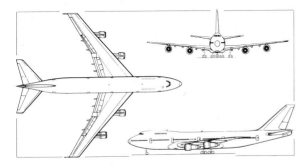

Power plant: Four General Electric F103-GE-100 turbofan engines (each 52 500 lb; 23 815 kg st)
Wing span: 195 ft 8 in (59.64 m)
Length overall: 231 ft 10 in (70.66 m)
Max T-O weight: approx 800 000 lb (362 870 kg)
Max level speed: at 30 000 ft (9 150 m), at AUW of 600 000 lb (272 155 kg): approx 528 knots (608 mph; 978 km/h)

Cruise ceiling: 45 000 ft (13 715 m)
Unrefuelled endurance: 12 h
Accommodation: E-4A has 4 620 sq ft (429.2 m²) of floor space, enabling it to accommodate almost three times the payload of the EC-135. Main deck is divided into six areas: NCA (National Command Authorities) work area, conference room, briefing room, battle staff work area, communications control centre, and flight crew rest area. Lobe areas beneath main deck house a technical control facility and limited onboard maintenance storage. E-4A can accommodate larger battle staff than EC-135; E-4B carries larger battle staff than E-4A
Operational equipment: E-4A fitted initially with equipment transferred from EC-135s, as interim measure. E-4B has 1 200kVA electrical system to support advanced data processing, communications equipment and other avionics. Details of these are classified, but suppliers include E-Systems, Collins, RCA, Burroughs, and Electrospace Systems
Variants:
E-4A: Three development aircraft, converted from commercial 747-200B with interim equipment. Currently (1980-81) capable of operating as National Emergency Airborne Command Posts (NEACPs). To be brought up to E-4B standard (1980 contract covers first conversion, with options for remaining two)
E-4B: Operational version, to replace EC-135 in airborne command post role. Identifiable by large, bulbous SHF (super high frequency) antenna fairing above and to rear of flight deck
In service with: US Air Force (planned force of six); first aircraft entered service January 1980

Flight refuelling tanker (KC-135), airborne command post/communications relay (EC-135) or electronics or photo reconnaissance (RC-135) aircraft

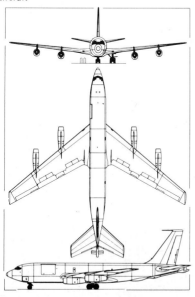

Photo: RC-135U for special reconnaissance
Drawing and Data: KC-135A Stratotanker

Power plant: Four Pratt & Whitney J57-P-59W turbojet engines (each 13 750 lb; 6 237 kg st)
Wing span: 130 ft 10 in (39.88 m)
Length overall: 136 ft 3 in (41.53 m)
Max T-O weight: 297 000 lb (134 715 kg)
Average cruising speed: at 30 500-45 000 ft (9 300-13 700 m): 462 knots (532 mph; 856 km/h)
Max rate of climb at S/L: 1 290 ft (393 m)/min
Service ceiling: 50 000 ft (15 240 m)
Transfer radius: with 6 734 lb (3 055 kg) fuel reserve: 1 000 nm (1 150 miles; 1 850 km)
Variants (excluding transports and testbeds):
C-135F: Flight refuelling tanker for French Mirage IV; refit with CFM56 engines planned
EC-135A: SAC command post and communications relay; Pratt & Whitney J57-P-59W engines
EC-135C/J: SAC command post and communications relay; TF33-P-9 turbofan engines
EC-135G/H/K/L/P: command post and communications relay versions
EC-135N: Electronic advanced range instrumentation version for Apollo programme
KC-135A: Flight refuelling tanker for Strategic Air Command bombers of the USAF. Also used as passenger or cargo transport
KC-135D: Former RC-135A photo-recce/mapping aircraft, now converted to tanker

(cont on page 45)

First flight 1956

BREGUET ALIZÉ (France)

Three-seat carrier-borne anti-submarine aircraft

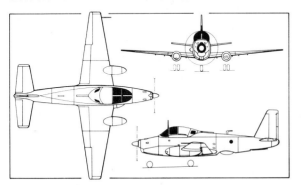

Power plant: One Rolls-Royce Dart RDa 7 Mk 21 turboprop engine (2 100 ehp)
Wing span: 51 ft 2 in (15.60 m)
Length: 45 ft 5¾ in (13.86 m)
Max T-O weight: 18 078 lb (8 200 kg)
Max speed at 10 000 ft (3 050 m): 253 knots (292 mph; 470 km/h)
Rate of climb at S/L: 1 380 ft (420 m)/min
Service ceiling: over 20 500 ft (6 250 m)
Normal range: 1 345 nm (1 550 miles; 2 500 km)
Armament: Weapon bay accommodates a torpedo or three 160 kg depth charges. Racks for two 160 kg or 175 kg depth charges under inner wings and for six 5 in rockets or two AS.12 missiles under outer wings. Sonobuoys inside front of wheel fairings
In service with: Navies of France and India

Boeing KC-135 *(cont from page 43)*
KC-135Q: Flight refuelling tanker for SR-71 reconnaissance aircraft
KC-135RE: Refit of KC-135A with 22 000 lb (9 980 kg) st CFM56 engines. Testbed evaluation 1980/81: plans to convert up to 100, for redelivery beginning in 1984
RC-135B: Electronic reconnaissance version
RC-135C/D/E/M/R/S/T/U/V/W: Electronic and special reconnaissance

versions; TF33-P-9 engines, various noses, external fairings and antennae. W similar to M, but refuelling boom deleted
WC-135B: Weather reconnaissance version
In service with: Air forces of France (C-135F) and USA (Air Force, KC-135A production version, of which some converted to EC-135A/G/H/K/L/P; EC-135C/J; RC-135A, now converted to KC-135D, and RC-135B, of which some converted to RC-135D/M/S

First flight 1961

Long-range maritime patrol aircraft

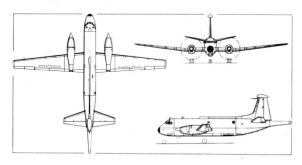

Power plant: Two SNECMA-built Rolls-Royce Tyne RTy 20 Mk 21 turboprop engines (each 6 106 ehp)
Wing span: 119 ft 1 in (36.30 m)
Length overall: 104 ft 2 in (31.75 m)
Max T-O weight: 95 900 lb (43 500 kg)
Max level speed: at high altitudes: 355 knots (409 mph; 658 km/h)

Service ceiling: 32 800 ft (10 000 m)
Max range: 4 854 nm (5 590 miles; 9 000 km)
Accommodation: Normal crew of 12 (pilot, co-pilot, flight engineer, three observers, radio-navigator, ESM/ECM/MAD operator, radar-IFF operator, tactical co-ordinator, and two acoustic sensor operators). Provision for relief crew or 12 other personnel
Armament: Main weapons carried in fuselage bay. Weapons include all NATO standard bombs, 175 kg French or 385 lb US depth charges, HVAR rockets, homing torpedoes, including types such as the Mk 44 Brush or LX 4 with acoustic heads, or four underwing air-to-surface missiles with nuclear or HE warheads
Variants:
Atlantic: Standard current version as described above. Five of the aircraft supplied to Germany have been converted for special-purpose ECM duties
Atlantic ANG (Atlantic Nouvelle Génération). Derivative of original Atlantic, under development by Dassault-Breguet as potential French Navy replacement for Atlantic and Neptune between 1985-90; prototype flown 8 May 1981. Main changes are structural (to prolong airframe life and improve maintenance), plus later-generation avionics and weapons.
In service with: Navies of France, German Federal Republic, Italy and Netherlands, and Pakistan Air Force

CANADAIR CL-41/CT-114 TUTOR (Canada)

Side-by-side two-seat light attack aircraft (CL-41G) and jet basic trainer (CT-114)

Photo and Data: CL-41G Tebuan
Drawing: CT-114 Tutor

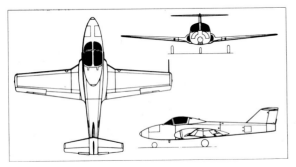

Power plant: One General Electric J85-J4 turbojet engine (2 950 lb; 1 340 kg st)
Wing span: 36 ft 5.9 in (11.13 m)
Length overall: 32 ft 0 in (9.75 m)
Max T-O weight: 11 288 lb (5 131 kg)
Max level speed: at 28 500 ft (8 700 m) with 50% fuel and no external stores: 417 knots (480 mph; 774 km/h)
Service ceiling: 42 200 ft (12 800 m)
Max range: 1 163 nm (1 340 miles; 2 155 km) with six fuel tanks under the wings and centre-section
Armament: Up to 4 000 lb (1 815 kg) of gun pods, bombs, rockets and missiles can be carried externally
Current variants:
CT-114 Tutor: Canadian-built General Electric J85-Can-40 turbojet engine (2 633 lb; 1 195 kg st). First delivered October 1963
CL-41G: Light attack version and armed trainer
In service with: Air forces of Canada (CT-114 Tutor) and Malaysia (CL-41G Tebuan)

First flight 1957

CANADAIR CP-107 ARGUS (Canada)

Long-range maritime patrol aircraft

Photo, Drawing and Data: CP-107 Argus Mk 2

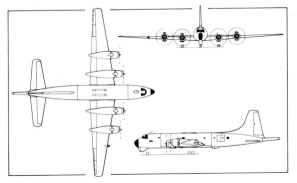

Power plant: Four Wright R-3350 (TC18EA1) Turbo Compound engines (each 3 700 hp)
Wing span: 142 ft 3½ in (43.37 m)
Length overall: 128 ft 3 in (39.09 m)
Max T-O weight: 148 000 lb (67 130 kg)
Max level speed: 273 knots (315 mph; 507 km/h)
Service ceiling: over 20 000 ft (6 100 m)
Range: over 3 475 nm (4 000 miles; 6 440 km) for patrol duties
Accommodation: Normal crew of 15 (three pilots, three navigators, two flight engineers and seven communications/avionics operators)
Armament: Two bomb bays each can accommodate 4 000 lb (1 815 kg) of stores, including homing torpedoes. Provision for carrying 3 800 lb (1 724 kg) of weapons under each outer wing
Variants:
Argus Mk 1: Initial production version; large chin radome housing American APS-20 search radar
Argus Mk 2: Smaller chin radome housing new equipment including British ASV-21 radar. Production completed July 1960
In service with: Canadian Armed Forces

Side-by-side two-seat light attack aircraft (A-37) and jet basic trainer (T-37)

Photo, Drawing and Data: A-37B Dragonfly

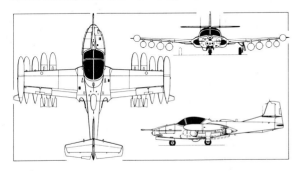

Power plant: Two General Electric J85-GE-17A turbojet engines (each 2 850 lb; 1 293 kg st)
Wing span: 35 ft 10½ in (10.93 m) over tip-tanks
Length overall: 28 ft 3¼ in (8.62 m), excl refuelling probe
Max T-O weight: 14 000 lb (6 350 kg)
Max level speed: at 16 000 ft (4 875 m): 440 knots (507 mph; 816 km/h)
Rate of climb at S/L: 6 990 ft (2 130 m)/min

Service ceiling: 41 765 ft (12 730 m)
Range with max payload: incl 4 100 lb (1 860 kg) ordnance: 399 nm (460 miles; 740 km)
Armament: GAU-2B/A 7.62 mm Minigun in forward fuselage. Each wing has four pylon stations, the two inner ones carrying 870 lb (394 kg) each, the intermediate one 600 lb (272 kg) and the outer one 500 lb (227 kg). The following weapons, in various combinations, can be carried on the underwing pylons: SUU-20 bomb and rocket pod, Mk 81 or Mk 82 bomb, BLU-32/B fire bomb, SUU-11/A gun pod, CBU-24/B or CBU-25/A dispenser and bomb, M117 demolition bomb, LAU-3/A rocket pod, CBU-12/A, CBU-14/A, or CBU-22/A dispenser and bomb, BLU-1C/B fire bomb, LAU-32/A or LAU-59/A rocket pod, CBU-19/A canister cluster and SUU-25/A flare launcher
Variants:
A-37A: Interim attack version, converted from T-37B
A-37B: Main production attack version
T-37A: Initial production trainer; two Continental J69-T-9 turbojets. Converted to T-37B
T-37B: Improved trainer: Continental J69-T-25 turbojet engines (each 1 025 lb; 465 kg st). New Omni navigational equipment, etc
T-37C. Similar to T-37B but with provision for armament and wing-tip fuel tanks
In service with: Air forces of Burma (T-37C), Chile (T-37B, T-37C and A-37B), Colombia (T-37C), Ecuador (A-37B), German Federal Republic (T-37B, based in the USA), Greece (T-37C), Guatemala (A-37B and T-37C), Honduras (A-37B), Jordan (T-37C), Kampuchea (T-37B), Pakistan (T-37B and T-37C), Paraguay (A-37B), Peru (A-37B, T-37B and T-37C), Portugal (T-37C), Thailand (A-37B, T-37B and T-37C), Turkey (T-37C), USA (T-37A/B and A-37B Dragonfly), Uruguay (A-37B), and Viet-Nam (A-37, ex-USAF)

CONVAIR F-106 DELTA DART (USA)

Single-seat interceptor fighter (F-106A) and two-seat combat trainer (F-106B)

Photo, Drawing and Data: F-106A Delta Dart

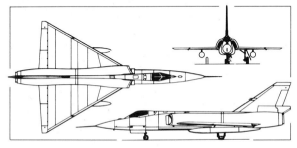

Power plant: One Pratt & Whitney J75-P-17 turbojet engine (24 500 lb; 11 113 kg st with afterburning)
Wing span: 38 ft 3½ in (11.67 m)
Length overall: 70 ft 8¾ in (21.56 m)
Max T-O weight: over 35 000 lb (15 875 kg)
Max level speed at 36 000 ft (11 000 m): Mach 2.3 (1 324 knots; 1 525 mph; 2 455 km/h)
Max rate of climb at S/L: approx 30 000 ft (9 145 m)/min
Service ceiling: 57 000 ft (17 375 m)
Range: 998 nm (1 150 miles; 1 850 km)
Armament: One AIR-2A Genie nuclear-warhead rocket, four Hughes AIM-4F or AIMd4G Super Falcon air-to-air missiles in internal weapon bay. One 20 mm M61A1 cannon in most aircraft
Variants:
F-106A: Standard single-seat interceptor version; production ended in 1961
F-106B: Armed tandem two-seat trainer version
In service with: US Air Force (F-106A and F-106B)

Single-seat carrier-based strike fighter (IV-M and Super Étendard) and tactical reconnaissance aircraft/tanker (IV-P)

Photo, Drawing and Data: Super Étendard

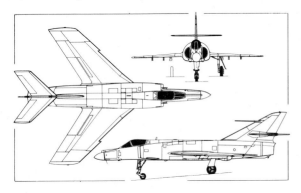

Power plant: One SNECMA Atar 8K-50 turbojet engine (11 023 lb; 5 000 kg st)

Wing span: 31 ft 6 in (9.60 m)
Length overall: 46 ft 11½ in (14.31 m)
Max T-O weight: 26 455 lb (12 000 kg)
Max level speed at low altitude: 650 knots (748 mph; 1 204 km/h)
Service ceiling: 45 000 ft (13 700 m)
Combat radius: with AM39 missile: 390 nm (450 miles; 720 km)
Armament: Two 30 mm DEFA cannon (each with 125 rds). Underfuselage attachments for two 250 kg bombs. Four underwing attachments for 400 kg bombs, Magic air-to-air missiles, or rocket pods. Optionally, one Exocet AM39 air-to-surface missile under starboard wing, and one auxiliary fuel tank under port wing
Variants:
IV-M: Initial fighter version with folding wings, long-stroke undercarriage, fittings for catapulting, deck arrester hook, retractable refuelling probe, a high-lift flap system, and Aida 7 fire control radar; some equipped as 'buddy' tankers. SNECMA Atar 8B turbojet engine (9 700 lb; 4 400 kg st)
IV-P: Reconnaissance and tanker version with five Omera cameras in nose and ventral positions. No armament
Super Étendard: Transonic single-seat strike fighter, for low and medium altitude operations from ships of the *Clémenceau* and *Foch* class. Very comprehensive high-lift devices for shipboard use. Equipment includes highly sophisticated and accurate nav/attack integrated avionics. Deliveries began in June 1978
In service with: Naval air arms of Argentina (Super Étendard) and France (Étendard IV-M, IV-P and Super Étendard)

Single-seat fighter-bomber (III-C/E/O/S) and tactical reconnaissance aircraft (III-R); two-seat combat trainer (III-B/D)

Photo, Drawing and Data: Mirage III-E

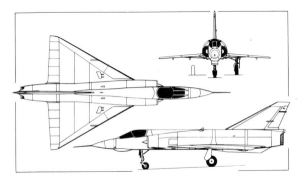

Power plant: One SNECMA Atar 9C turbojet engine (13 670 lb; 6 200 kg st with afterburning); optional and jettisonable SEPR 844 rocket motor (3 300 lb; 1 500 kg st)
Wing span: 26 ft 11½ in (8.22 m)
Length overall: 49 ft 3½ in (15.03 m)
Max T-O weight: 30 200 lb (13 700 kg)
Max level speed at 39 375 ft (12 000 m): Mach 2.2 (1 268 knots; 1 460 mph; 2 350 km/h)

Time to 36 000 ft (11 000 m), Max 0.9: 3 min
Service ceiling at Mach 1.8: 55 775 ft (17 000 m)
Ceiling, using rocket motor: 75 450 ft (23 000 m)
Combat radius, ground attack: 647 nm (745 miles; 1 200 km)
Armament: Ground attack armament consists normally of two 30 mm DEFA cannon in fuselage (125 rds each) and two 1 000 lb bombs, or an AS.30 air-to-surface missile under fuselage and 1 000 lb bombs under the wings. Alternative underwing stores include JL-100 pods, each with 18 rockets and additional fuel; two Bidon Cyclope or Bidon Homing fuel/avionics pods; or two conventional drop-tanks. For interception duties, one Matra R 530 air-to-air missile can be carried under fuselage, with optional guns and two Sidewinder missiles
Variants (see note at end of Mirage 5/50 entry):
III-B: Tandem two-seat trainer
III-BE: Tandem two-seat version of III-E
III-C: All-weather interceptor and day ground attack fighter. SNECMA Atar 9B turbojet
III-D: Tandem two-seat version of III-O
III-D2Z: For South Africa. Generally similar to III-D but with Atar 9K-50 engine (15 873 lb; 7 200 kg st)
III-E: Long-range fighter-bomber/intruder version. Longer by 11.8 in (30 cm) than III-C
III-O: III-E built under licence in Australia for fighter (III-OF) and attack (III-OA) duties
III-R: Reconnaissance version with five Omera type 31 cameras in modified nose
III-R2Z: For South Africa. Generally similar to III-R but with Atar 9K-50 engine

(cont on page 61)

Dassault Mirage IV-A

First flight 1959

DASSAULT MIRAGE IV-A (France)

Two-seat supersonic strategic bomber

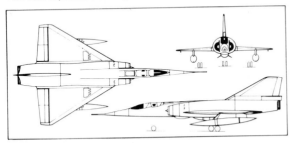

Wing span: 38 ft 10½ in (11.85 m)
Length overall: 77 ft 1¼ in (23.50 m)
Average T-O weight: 69 665 lb (31 600 kg)
Max level dash speed at 36 000 ft (11 000 m): Mach 2.2 (1 262 knots; 1 454 mph; 2 340 km/h)
Max level sustained speed at 60 000 ft (18 290 m): Mach 1.85 (1 061 knots; 1 222 mph; 1 966 km/h)
Time to 36 000 ft (11 000 m): 4 min 15 s
Service ceiling: 65 600 ft (20 000 m)
Tactical radius: 668 nm (770 miles; 1 240 km)
Armament: One 60 kiloton free-fall nuclear weapon semi-recessed under fuselage; or 16 × 1 000 lb bombs or four Martel air-to-surface missiles under wings and fuselage
In service with: French Air Force

Power plant: Two SNECMA Atar 9K-50 turbojet engines (each 15 873 lb; 7 200 kg st with afterburning)

Dassault Mirage III *(cont from page 59)*
III-RD: Similar to III-R but with improved Doppler navigation system
III-S: Developed from III-E, with a Hughes TARAN fire control system and armament of HM-55 Falcon missiles
See also IAI Kfir and Nesher

In service with: Air forces of Argentina (III-D and III-E), Australia (III-D and III-O), Brazil (III-D and III-E), France (III-B, III-BE, III-C, III-E, III-R and III-RD), Israel (III-B and III-C), Lebanon (III-D and III-E), Pakistan (III-D, III-E and III-R), South Africa (III-B, III-C, III-D/D2Z, III-E and III-R/R2Z), Spain (III-D and III-E), Switzerland (III-B, III-R and III-S) and Venezuela (III-E)

First flights 1967 (5), 1979 (50)

DASSAULT MIRAGE 5 and 50 (France)

Single-seat fighter-bomber and reconnaissance aircraft; two-seat combat trainer

Photo: Mirage 50
Drawing and Data: Mirage 5A

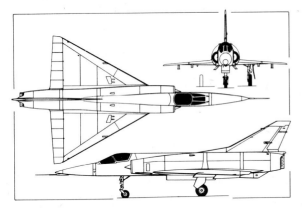

Power plant: One SNECMA Atar 9C turbojet engine (13 670 lb; 6 200 kg st with afterburning)
Wing span: 26 ft 11½ in (8.22 m)
Length overall: 51 ft 0¼ in (15.55 m)
Max T-O weight: 30 200 lb (13 700 kg)

Max level speed at 39 375 ft (12 000 m): Mach 2.2 (1 268 knots; 1 460 mph; 2 350 km/h)
Time to 36 000 ft (11 000 m), Mach 0.9: 3 min
Service ceiling at Mach 1.8: 55 775 ft (17 000 m)
Combat radius with 2 000 lb (907 kg) bomb load: hi-lo-hi: 700 nm (808 miles; 1 300 km); lo-lo-lo: 350 nm (404 miles; 650 km)
Armament: Ground attack armament consists normally of two 30 mm DEFA cannon in fuselage (125 rds each), and two 1 000 lb bombs or an AS.30 air-to-surface missile under fuselage and 1 000 lb bombs under wings. Alternative underwing stores include tank/bomb carriers, each with fuel and four 500 lb or two 1 000 lb bombs, and JL-100 pods, each with 18 × 68 mm rockets and 55 Imp gallons (250 litres) of fuel. For interception duties, two Sidewinder missiles can be carried under the wings
*Variants:
5A: Basic single-seat fighter-bomber/ground attack version
5D: Tandem two-seat trainer
5R: Single-seat reconnaissance version with cameras in modified nose
Mirage 50: Multi-mission version, powered by Atar 9K-50 engine of 15 873 lb (7 200 kg) st
Mirage 50D: Tandem two-seat trainer
In service with: Air forces of Abu Dhabi (5-AD/EAD, 5-DAD and 5-RAD), Belgium (5-BA, 5-BR and 5-BD), Chile (50C and 50DC), Colombia (5-COA, 5-COD and 5-COR), Egypt (5-SDE, 5-SDD and 5-SDR), France (5-F), Gabon (5-G and 5-DG), Libya (5-D/DD/DE/DR), Pakistan (5-PA), Peru (5-P and 5-DP), Venezuela (5-V and 5-DV) and Zaïre (5-M and 5-DM)

*Additional letter(s), added to designation to denote country of use, as indicated under 'In service with' heading

First flight 1966

DASSAULT MIRAGE F1 (France)

Single-seat all-weather multi-purpose fighter

Photo: Mirage F1-C-200
Drawing and Data: Mirage F1-C

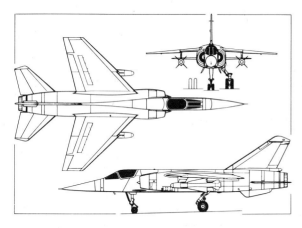

Power plant: One SNECMA Atar 9K-50 turbojet engine (15 873 lb; 7 200 kg st with afterburning)
Wing span: 27 ft 6¾ in (8.40 m)
Length overall: 49 ft 2½ in (15.00 m)

Max T-O weight: 33 510 lb (15 200 kg)
Max level speed: high altitude: Mach 2.2 (1 268 knots; 1 460 mph; 2 350 km/h); low altitude: Mach 1.2 (792 knots; 912 mph; 1 468 km/h)
Max rate of climb with afterburning: at S/L: 41 930 ft (12 780 m)/min; at high altitude: 47 835 ft (14 580 m)/min
Service ceiling: 65 600 ft (20 000 m)
Endurance: 3 h 45 min
Armament: Two 30 mm DEFA 553 cannon in lower front fuselage (125 rds each). Two Alkan universal stores attachment pylons under each wing and one under centre-fuselage, plus provision for carrying one air-to-air missile at each wingtip. Max external combat load 8 820 lb (4 000 kg). Externally-mounted weapons for interception role include Matra R 530 or Super 530 radar homing or infra-red homing air-to-air missiles on underfuselage and inboard wing pylons, and/or a Sidewinder or Matra 550 Magic infra-red homing air-to-air missile at each wingtip station. For ground attack duties, typical loads may include one AS.37 Martel anti-radar missile or AS.30 air-to-surface missile, eight 450 kg bombs, four launchers each containing 18 air-to-ground rockets, or six 132 Imp gallon (600 litre) napalm tanks
Variants:
F1-A: Ground attack version for operation only under VFR conditions, with much of the more costly avionics deleted and replaced by extra fuel tank
F1-B: Tandem two-seat operational trainer, first flown in May 1976
F1-C: Initial production version, primarily for all-weather, all-altitude interception

(cont on page 67)

Dassault Mirage 2000

First flight 1978

DASSAULT MIRAGE 2000 (France)

Single-seat interceptor and air superiority fighter; two-seat trainer

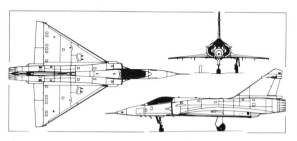

Power plant: One SNECMA M53-5 turbofan engine (19 840 lb; 9 000 kg st with afterburning) in initial production version; M53-P2 (21 385 lb; 9 700 kg st) under development for later use
Wing span: 29 ft 6 in (9.00 m)
Length overall: 50 ft 3½ in (15.33 m)
Combat T-O weight (estimated): 19 840 lb (9 000 kg)
Max level speed: above Mach 2.3
Max sustained speed: Mach 2.2

Rate of climb at S/L: 49 200 ft (15 000 m)/min
Time to 50 000 ft (15 250 m) and Mach 2: 4 min
Service ceiling: 65 600 ft (20 000 m)
Ferry range with external tanks: 2 100 nm (2 420 miles; 3 900 km)
Armament: Two 30 mm DEFA cannon in lower front fuselage. Five underfuselage attachments and two under each wing. Typical interception weapons comprise two Matra Super 530 missiles (inboard) and two Matra 550 Magic missiles (outboard) under wings. Strike version will carry up to 12 785 lb (5 800 kg) of external stores, including nuclear weapons such as ASMP
Variants:
Selected as primary combat aircraft of French Air Force from mid-1980s. Being developed initially for interception and air superiority; will be equally suitable for reconnaissance, close support, and low-altitude attack in areas to the rear of a battlefield. Five prototypes built, including one two-seat trainer version. Deliveries of production aircraft due to start in 1983. Prototypes of two-seat low-altitude penetration version scheduled to fly in 1983, with deliveries following from 1986
In production for: French Air Force (20 ordered by early 1981: initial requirement is for 127 air defence aircraft, possibly rising to 200; up to 200 more may be required eventually for reconnaissance/strike duties)

Dassault Mirage F-1 *(cont from page 65)*
F1-C-200. Designation of 25 French Air Force F1-Cs with in-flight refuelling probe installed permanently forward of windscreen
F1-E: Multi-mission version, similar to F1-C but with more comprehensive nav/attack system
F1-R: Reconnaissance version, with two photoflash containers and

a recce pod incorporating an SAT Cyclope infra-red system and EMI side-looking radar
In service with: Air forces of Ecuador (F1-A and F1-E), France (F1-B, F1-C, F1-C-200 and F1-R), Greece (F1-C), Iraq (F1-C), Jordan (F1-E), Kuwait (F1-B and F1-C), Libya (F1-A, F1-B and F1-E), Morocco (F1-C), South Africa (F1-A and F1-C), and Spain (F1-B and F1-C)

First flight 1979

DASSAULT SUPER MIRAGE 4000 (France)

Single-seat multi-role combat aircraft; two-seat version under study in 1980/81

Data: Prototype (provisional)

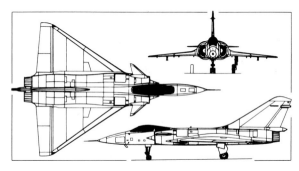

Power plant: Two SNECMA M53 turbofan engines (each approx 22 045 lb; 10 000 kg st with afterburning)
Wing span: 39 ft 4½ in (12.00 m)

Length overall: 61 ft 4¼ in (18.70 m)
T-O weight: approx 44 000 lb (20 000 kg) for early flight tests
Performance: Generally classified, but installation of two engines of the type fitted in the single-engined Mirage 2000 (which see) will give a power:weight ratio well above 1:1 in an interceptor role. Overall performance claimed to be superior to that of any aircraft in its class known to be in production or under development. Prototype achieved Mach 2.2 on its sixth test flight in April 1979, when it was flown at angles of attack of up to 25°. Features of design include computer-derived aerodynamics, with a rearward CG made possible by a fly-by-wire active control system; foreplanes; 'teardrop' cockpit canopy; very large nose radome; and extensive use of weight-saving boron and carbonfibre composites. Provision for large jettisonable fuel tank under fuselage and each wing; fuel tankage in fin helps to give total capacity about three times that of Mirage 2000
Armament: Provision for two 30 mm DEFA cannon in bottom of air intake trunks. Rail under each outer wing for a Matra 550 Magic air-to-air missile, plus a wide range of air-to-air and air-to-surface weapons. Total of 11 hardpoints for external stores, including drop-tanks
Variants:
Intended primarily for interception and low-altitude penetration attacks on targets a considerable distance from its base
Status: Under development with private funding; no orders announced up to early 1981

First flight 1955

Single-seat interceptor and tactical strike fighter

Photo and Drawing: Super Mystère with J52-P-8A turbojet engine
Data: Super Mystère B-2 with original Atar engine

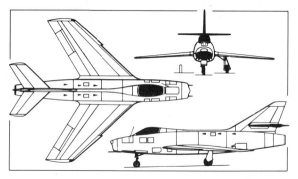

Power plant: One SNECMA Atar 101G turbojet engine (9 920 lb; 4 500 kg st with afterburning)

DASSAULT SUPER MYSTÈRE B-2 (France)

Wing span: 34 ft 5¾ in (10.51 m)
Length overall: 46 ft 1 in (14.04 m)
Max T-O weight: 22 045 lb (10 000 kg)
Max level speed at 36 000 ft (11 000 m): Mach 1.125 (645 knots; 743 mph; 1 195 km/h)
Rate of climb: at 19 840 lb (9 000 kg) AUW: 17 500 ft (5 340 m)/min
Service ceiling: 55 775 ft (17 000 m)
Normal range: 520 nm (600 miles; 965 km)
Armament: Two 30 mm DEFA cannon and a pack of air-to-air rockets in fuselage. Underwing loads are made up of 38 rockets in two packs, or two 500 kg bombs, two napalm tanks, 12 air-to-surface rockets or two Matra air-to-air guided missiles
Variants:
B-2: Production version, the last being delivered in 1959
B-4: Test aircraft, fitted with the SNECMA Atar 9 turbojet engine and first flown on 9 February 1958
In service with: Air forces of El Salvador and Honduras (ex-Israeli B-2s re-engined with 9 300 lb; 4 218 kg st non-afterburning Pratt & Whitney J52-P-8A turbojets and having other improvements to airframe, avionics and weapons capability)

71

Tandem two-seat close support and battlefield reconnaissance aircraft (Alpha Jet A) and basic/low-altitude/advanced jet trainer (Alpha Jet E)

Photo and Data: Alpha Jet A

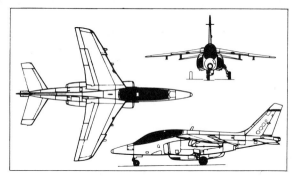

Power plant: Two SNECMA/Turboméca Larzac 04-C5 turbofan engines (each 2 976 lb; 1 350 kg st)
Wing span: 29 ft 10¾ in (9.11 m)
Length overall: 43 ft 5 in (13.23 m) incl probe
Max T-O weight: 16 535 lb (7 500 kg)

Max level speed, 'clean' T-O weight of 11 023 lb (5 000 kg): at S/L: 540 knots (622 mph; 1 000 km/h); at 32 800 ft (10 000 m): 488 knots (562 mph; 904 km/h)
Max rate of climb at S/L, T-O weight as above: 11 220 ft (3 420 m)/min
Service ceiling, T-O weight as above: 48 000 ft (14 630 m)
Combat radius (incl 5 min combat) with belly gun pod, underwing weapons and external tanks: lo-lo-lo: 305 nm (351 miles; 565 km); hi-lo-hi: 555 nm (639 miles; 1 028 km)
Armament: Can be equipped with underfuselage detachable pod containing a 30 mm DEFA or 27 mm Mauser cannon with 150 rds. Provision also for two hardpoints under each wing, on which can be carried various combinations of 50, 125, 250 or 400 kg HE or retarded bombs; 625 lb cluster dispensers; 690 or 825 lb special-purpose tanks; adaptors for 6 to 18 rockets and four practice bombs, or one 500 lb bomb, or 6 penetration bombs, or grenades or other stores; Dassault-Breguet 30 mm gun pods; pods of 18 × 68 mm rockets; Magic air-to-air or Maverick air-to-surface missiles; reconnaissance pod; or drop-tanks. Total load (five stations) 5 510 lb (2 500 kg)
Variants:
Alpha Jet A: Close support version, as described
Alpha Jet E: Trainer version; those of Belgian Air Force known as Alpha Jet 1B. Modified nose, with small strake each side; less comprehensive avionics, equipment and armament
In service with: Air forces of Belgium (E/1B), Egypt (E on order), France (E), German Federal Republic (A), Ivory Coast (E), Morocco (E), Nigeria (E), Qatar (E) and Togo (E)

Single-seat fighter-bomber

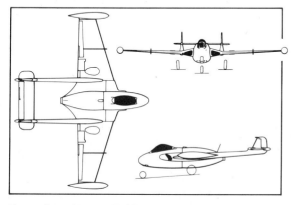

Photo: Swiss Venom FB Mk 50 with uprated avionics in re-contoured nose

Drawing: Venom FB Mk 4
Data: Venom FB Mk 50 except where indicated
Power plant: One de Havilland Ghost 103 turbojet engine (4 850 lb; 2 200 kg st)
Wing span: 41 ft 8 in (12.70 m)
Length overall: 33 ft 10¾ in (10.33 m)
Max T-O weight: 15 400 lb (6 985 kg)
Max level speed: 564 knots (649 mph; 1 045 km/h)
Max rate of climb at S/L: FB Mk 4: 7 230 ft (2 204 m)/min
Service ceiling: 49 200 ft (15 000 m)
Range with external tanks: over 868 nm (1 000 miles; 1 610 km)
Armament: Four 20 mm cannon in nose. Underwing stores totalling up to 2 000 lb (907 kg) including bombs and rockets
Variants:
FB Mk 1: Single-seat fighter version, produced originally for RAF; 150 built under licence in Switzerland as FB Mk 50
FB Mk 4: Developed version of FB Mk 1 with powered ailerons and redesigned tail
FB Mk 50: See above
In service with: Air force of Switzerland (FB Mk 4 and FB Mk 50)

Land-based maritime reconnaissance aircraft

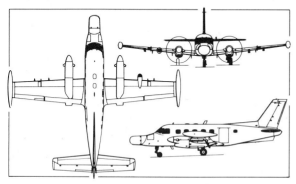

Power plant: Two Pratt & Whitney Aircraft of Canada PT6A-34 turboprop engines (each 750 shp)

Wing span: 52 ft 4 in (15.95 m) over tip-tanks
Length overall: 48 ft 11 in (14.91 m)
Max T-O weight: 15 432 lb (7 000 kg)
Max cruising speed at 10 000 ft (3 050 m): 208 knots (239 mph; 385 km/h)
Max rate of climb at S/L: 1 190 ft (362 m)/min
Service ceiling at AUW of 11 684 lb (5 300 kg): 25 500 ft (7 770 m)
Max range: 1 590 nm (1 830 miles; 2 945 km)
Accommodation: Pilot and co-pilot side by side on flight deck. Stations in cabin for search radar/radio operator, ECM operator, one or two observers, and a second radar or ECM operator. Port-side door at rear can be used for loading freight, and for airdropping personnel and survival equipment
Armament: Four underwing pylons for eight 5 in air-to-surface rockets (two per pylon), or four seven-round packs of 2.75 in rockets; or three pylons, plus a searchlight on the leading-edge of the starboard wing. Provision for smoke grenades, flares and chaff dispensers
In service with: Air forces of Brazil and Gabon, and Chilean Navy

First flight 1949

ENGLISH ELECTRIC CANBERRA (UK)

Three-seat tactical light bomber, interdictor/strike and photo-graphic reconnaissance aircraft

Photo: Canberra B Mk 62
Drawing: Canberra PR Mk 9
Data: Canberra B Mk 6

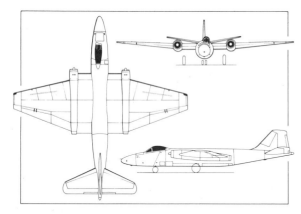

Power plant: Two Rolls-Royce Avon 109 turbojet engines (each 7 400 lb; 3 355 kg st)
Wing span: 63 ft 11½ in (19.50 m)
Length overall: 65 ft 6 in (19.96 m)

Max T-O weight: 55 000 lb (24 945 kg)
Max level speed at 30 000 ft (9.145 m): 504 knots (580 mph; 930 km/h)
Max rate of climb at S/L: 3 400 ft (1 036 m)/min
Service ceiling: 48 000 ft (14 630 m)
Ferry range: 3 290 nm (3 790 miles; 6 100 km)
Armament: In bomber role can carry 6 000 lb (2 720 kg) of weapons internally. Up to 2 000 lb (907 kg) of external stores including bombs, rocket pods or guided weapons can be carried on under-wing pylons on later, modified aircraft
Variants (UK only):
PR Mk 7: Photo-reconnaissance aircraft: seven cameras
PR Mk 9: High-altitude reconnaissance aircraft; Avon 206 turbojet engines (11 000 lb; 4 990 kg st each)
E Mk 15: Version for radar and radio calibration
T Mk 4: Dual-control trainer
T Mk 17: Electronic countermeasures trainer
TT Mk 18: Target tug
T Mk 19: Target conversion
T Mk 22: Radar target for Royal Navy
In service with: Air forces of Argentina (B Mk 62 and T Mk 64), Australia (B Mk 20 and T Mk 21), Ecuador (B Mk 6), Ethiopia (B Mk 52), India (PR Mk 57, B(I) Mk 58, B Mk 66, T Mks 54/67), Peru (B Mks 2/72, T Mks 4/74, B(I) Mk 8, B Mk 56 and B(I) Mk 78), South Africa (T Mk 4 and B(I) Mk 12), UK (Air Force T Mk 4, PR Mk 7, PR Mk 9, E Mk 15, T Mk 17, TT Mk 18, and T Mk 19; Navy TT Mk 18 and T Mk 22), Venezuela (B Mk 2, B(I) Mk 82, PR Mks 3/83, T Mks 4/84 and B(I) Mks 8/88) and Zimbabwe (B Mk 2 and T Mk 4)

See also Martin B-57

Single-seat close-support aircraft

Photo, Drawing and Data: A-10A Thunderbolt II

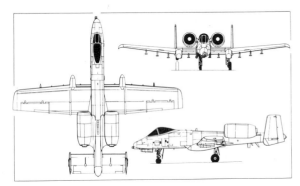

Power plant: Two General Electric TF34-GE-100 high bypass ratio turbofan engines (each 9 065 lb; 4 112 kg st)
Wing span: 57 ft 6 in (17.53 m)
Length overall: 53 ft 4 in (16.26 m)
Max T-O weight: 50 000 lb (22 680 kg)

Combat speed at 5 000 ft (1 525 m): 387 knots (446 mph; 717 km/h) with six Mk 82 bombs
Max rate of climb at S/L: 6 000 ft (1 828 m)/min
Operational radius (deep strike mission): 540 nm (620 miles; 1 000 km) plus 20 min reserves
Armament: General Electric GAU-8/A Avenger seven-barrel 30 mm gun (1 174 rds) in the nose. Four pylons under each wing, one inboard and three outboard of main-wheel fairing, and three under fuselage, for max external load of 16 000 lb (7 250 kg). The centre-line pylon and the two flanking fuselage pylons cannot be occupied simultaneously. Pylons allow carriage of a wide range of stores including 28 × 500 lb Mk-82 LDGP, 28 × 500 lb Mk 82 retarded or 6 × 2 000 lb Mk 84 general purpose bombs; 8 BLU-1 or BLU-27/B incendiary bombs; 4 SUU-25 flare launchers; 20 Rockeye II cluster bombs, 16 CBU-52/71 dispenser weapons; 6 AGM-65A Maverick missiles; Mk 82 and Mk 84 laser-guided bombs; Mk 84 EO-guided bombs; 2 SUU-23 gun pods; chaff, ECM or other jammer pods; or three drop-tanks
Variants:
A-10A. Standard production version, as described
Night/Adverse Weather A-10. Two-seat attack version, with secondary use as combat-capable operational trainer. Company-funded prototype first flown May 1979; evaluation continuing in 1980/81. Rear seat occupied by weapons system officer, freeing pilot of responsibility for ECM, navigation, target/threat acquisition and designation. Radar and FLIR carried in lengthened mainwheel fairings; height of tail-fins increased; multi-mode radar and other improved avionics
In service with: US Air Force (A-10A)

Single-seat tactical fighter-bomber (F-105D); two-seat fighter-bomber/operational trainer (F-105F) and ground defence suppression aircraft (F-105G)

Photo: F-105G Thunderchief
Drawing and Data: F-105D Thunderchief

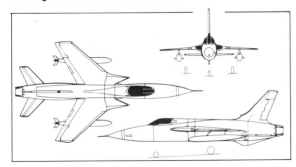

Power plant: One Pratt & Whitney J75-P-19W turbojet engine (26 500 lb; 12 030 kg st with water injection and afterburning)
Wing span: 34 ft 11.2 in (10.65 m)
Length overall: 67 ft 0¼ in (20.43 m)
Max T-O weight: 52 840 lb (23 968 kg)
Max level speed at 36 000 ft (11 000 m): Mach 2.1 (1 202 knots; 1 385 mph; 2 230 km/h)
Max level speed at S/L: Mach 1.125 (742 knots; 855 mph; 1 375 km/h)

Typical rate of climb at S/L: 34 500 ft (10 515 m)/min
Service ceiling: 52 000 ft (15 850 m)
Range with max fuel: approx 1 797 nm (2 070 miles; 3 330 km)
Armament: One General Electric M61 Vulcan automatic multi-barrel 20 mm gun (1,029 rds) in port side of nose. Over 14 000 lb (6 350 kg) of internal and external stores can be carried. Typical alternative loads are: (1) 650 gal centreline tank, 450 gal tank on one inner wing pylon, nuclear store on other inner pylon; (2) 450 gal tanks on centreline and inner wing pylons, nuclear weapon in bomb bay; (3) 650 gal centreline tank, two 3 000 lb bombs on inner wing pylons; (4) 650 gal centreline tank, two 450 gal tanks on inner wing pylons, four Sidewinder missiles on outer wing pylons; (5) three rocket packs on centreline, two on each inner wing pylon and one on each outer pylon; (6) nine BLU-1/B fire bombs or nine MLU-10/B mines in similar arrangement to rocket packs, or sixteen leaflet bombs, 750 lb bombs, or MC-1 toxic bombs. Adaptation of F-105 to carry-then new missiles carried out during early 1970s
Variants:
F-105D: All-weather tactical fighter-bomber
F-105F: Tandem two-seat combat/trainer. Length 69 ft 1.18 in (21.06 m) and max T-O weight 54 000 lb (24 495 kg). Other changes include a higher vertical tail
F-105G: Two-seat 'Wild Weasel' ECM and ground defence suppression aircraft, converted from F-105F. Used during Viet-Nam war against anti-aircraft missile sites. ECM pod on fuselage, four AGM-45 Shrike or two AGM-78 Standard ARM anti-radiation missiles
In service with: US Air Force Reserve and Air National Guard (F-105D, including several with 'T-Stick II' bombing system in saddleback fairing, F-105F and F-105G)

First flight 1969

Tandem two-seat counter-insurgency aircraft

Photo, Drawing and Data: IA 58A Pucará

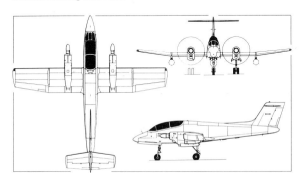

Power plant: Two Turboméca Astazou XVIG turboprop engines (each 1 022 ehp)

Wing span: 47 ft 6¾ in (14.50 m)
Length overall: 46 ft 9 in (14.25 m)
Max T-O weight: 14 991 lb (6 800 kg)
Max level speed at 9 845 ft (3 000 m): 270 knots (310 mph; 500 km/h)
Max rate of climb at S/L: 3 543 ft (1 080 m)/min
Service ceiling: 32 810 ft (10 000 m)
Range with max fuel at 16 400 ft (5 000 m): 1 641 nm (1 890 miles; 3 042 km)
Armament: Two 20 mm Hispano HS-2804 cannon (each with 270 rds) and four 7.62 mm FN-Browning machine-guns (each with 900 rds) in fuselage. Max external load of 3 571 lb (1 620 kg) of external gun pods, rocket pods, bombs or auxiliary fuel tanks, carried on Aero 7A-1 underfuselage centreline pylon (capacity 2 205 lb; 1 000 kg) and two Aero 20A-1 pylons (each of 1 102 lb; 500 kg capacity), one under each outer wing. Matra 83-4-3 reflector gunsight and AN/AWE-1 programmer
Variants:
IA 58A: Initial production version, as described
IA 58B Pucará Bravo: Improved follow-on version, generally as IA 58A except for deeper forward fuselage, upgraded avionics, and 30 mm DEFA 553 cannon (each with 140 rds) replacing 20 mm Hispanos. First flown May 1979; to enter production in 1981
In service with: Argentinian Air Force (IA 58A; IA 58B on order)

Single-seat lightweight fighter (F-16A) and two-seat fighter-trainer (F-16B)

Photo and Data: F-16A Fighting Falcon
Drawing: F-16A Fighting Falcon

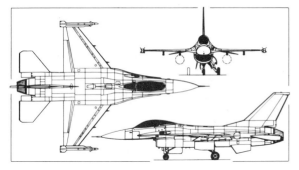

Power plant: One Pratt & Whitney F100-PW-200 turbofan engine (approx 25 000 lb; 11 340 kg st with afterburning)
Wing span: 31 ft 0 in (9.45 m) over missile launchers
Length overall: 47 ft 7.7 in (14.52 m), excl probe
Max T-O weight: 23 357 lb (10 594 kg) air-to-air mission with no external tanks; 35 400 lb (16 057 kg) with external load
Max level speed at 40 000 ft (12 200 m): over Mach 2 (1 147 knots; 1 320 mph; 2 125 km/h)

Service ceiling: over 50,000 ft (15 240 m)
Radius of action: over 500 nm (575 miles; 925 km)
Armament: One fuselage-mounted General Electric 20 mm M61A1 multi-barrel cannon (with 500 rds), and an infra-red missile mounted at each wingtip. Six underwing hardpoints and one under fuselage; max external load 15 200 lb (6 894 kg) with reduced internal fuel; with full internal fuel, approx 12 000 lb (5 443 kg) of external stores can be carried. Typical loads can include two wing-tip AIM-9J/L Sidewinders (plus four more underwing); an under-fuselage 2 200 lb bomb; Martin Marietta Pave Penny laser tracker pod along starboard side of engine nacelle; single or cluster bombs; air-to-surface missiles; flare pods; ALQ-119 and ALQ-131 jammer pods (centreline and two underwing stations); rockets; laser-guided and electro-optical weapons; and various sizes of drop-tank
Variants:
F-16A: Production single-seat fighter version; first flown in December 1976
F-16B: Tandem two-seat fighter-trainer version, with special avionics
F-16/79: Proposed export version with 18 000 lb (8 165 kg) st J79-GE-119 engine: first flown 29 October 1980
F-16/101: Testbed for General Electric F101 Derivative Fighter Engine, rated at 26,000-28,000 lb (11 800-12 700 kg) st. First flight 19 December 1980
AFTI-16: Testbed (converted F-16A) for advanced technology demonstration: ventral manoeuvring canard surfaces, dorsal avionics fairing. Due to fly in 1981
In service with (F-16A/B): Air forces of Belgium, Denmark, Egypt (on order), Israel, Netherlands, Norway and USA

First flight 1964

Side-by-side two-seat tactical fighter-bomber

Photo: F-111C
Drawing: F-111A
Data: F-111F

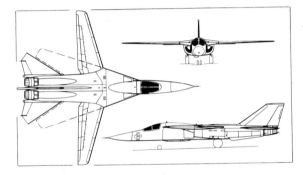

Power plant: Two Pratt & Whitney TF30-P-100 turbofan engines (each 25 100 lb; 11 385 kg st with afterburning)
Wing span: spread: 63 ft 0 in (19.20 m); fully swept: 31 ft 11.4 in (9.74 m). (F-111C has wing span of 70 ft 0 in; 21.34 m/33 ft 11 in; 10.34 m)
Length overall: 73 ft 6 in (22.40 m)

GENERAL DYNAMICS F-111 (USA)

Max T-O weight: 100 000 lb (45 360 kg)
Max level speed at height: Mach 2.5 (1 433 knots; 1 650 mph; 2 655 km/h)
Max level speed at S/L: Mach 1.2 (792 knots; 912 mph; 1 468 km/h)
Service ceiling: over 59 000 ft (18 000 m)
Range with max internal fuel: over 2 540 nm (2 925 miles; 4 707 km)
Armament: Three attachments under each wing, for a wide range of conventional and nuclear weapons, including the latest air-to-surface tactical weapons. Fuselage weapon bay for two 750 lb B43 bombs, or a 20 mm M61A1 multi-barrel cannon plus one B43, or a Ford Aerospace AN/AVQ-26 Pave Tack pod providing day/night all-weather capability to acquire, track and designate ground targets for laser, IR and EO guided weapons
Variants:
F-111A: Two-seat tactical fighter-bomber with 18 500 lb (8 390 kg) st TF30-P-3 engines and 'Mk I' avionics; approval for updated avionics, incl INS and new bombing/nav system, anticipated in FY 1981
EF-111A: ECM (jamming) conversion of F-111F, with AN/ALQ-99E jammers in ventral pack and receiver pod on top of fin. Developed by Grumman; first flown 1977. Deliveries of six to begin in mid-1981; conversion of 36 more envisaged
F-111C: Strike aircraft. Mk I avionics, cockpit ejection module. Eight underwing attachments for stores
RF-111C: Modified F-111C (four converted) for strike/reconnaissance, with vertical and high/low level panoramic cameras, infra-red linescan, and TV

(cont on page 91)

General Dynamics FB-111A

First flight 1967

GENERAL DYNAMICS FB-111 (USA)

Side-by-side two-seat strategic bomber

Photo, Drawing and Data: FB-111A

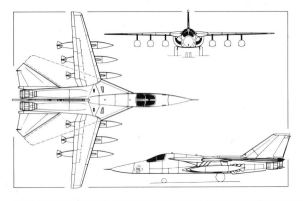

Power plant: Two Pratt & Whitney TF30-P-7 turbofan engines (each 20 350 lb; 9 240 kg st with afterburning)
Wing span: spread: 70 ft 0 in (21.34 m); fully swept: 33 ft 11 in (10.34 m)
Length overall: 73 ft 6 in (22.40 m)
Max T-O weight: approx 100 000 lb (45 360 kg)
Max level speed at height: Mach 2.5 (1 433 knots; 1 650 mph; 2 655 km/h)
Max level speed at S/L: Mach 1.2 (792 knots; 912 mph; 1 468 km/h)
Range: approx 3 474 nm (4 000 miles; 6 437 km)
Armament: 31 500 lb (14 288 kg) max load, comprising 42 × 750 lb bombs, of which two are carried in internal bay and 40 in clusters on eight underwing attachments. Full load is carried with wings swept at 26°, reducing to 32 bombs (six underwing attachments) at 54° of sweep, or 20 bombs at full sweep. Ability to carry six nuclear bombs or AGM-69A SRAM missiles or a combination of the two
Variants:
FB-111A: Initial version, as described
FB-111B/C: Proposed conversions (of F-111D and FB-111A respectively) with new engines in modified rear fuselage, increased wing span, and additional fuel capacity
In service with: US Air Force (FB-111A)

General Dynamics F-111 *(cont from page 89)*
F-111D: Similar to F-111A but with Mk II avionics, offering improvements in navigation and air-to-air weapon delivery and TF30-P-9 engines
F-111E: Modified air intakes to improve engine performance; approval for updated avionics, incl INS and new bombing/nav

system, anticipated in FY 1981
F-111F: Fighter-bomber. Generally similar to F-111D but with provisions for Pave Tack pod in weapons bay, and avionics that combine best features of F-111E and FB-111A systems
In service with: Air forces of Australia (F-111A, F-111C and RF-111C) and USA (F-111A, EF-111A, F-111D, F-111E and F-111F)

Side-by-side two-seat carrier-borne strike (A-6), electronic reconnaissance (EA-6A) and tanker aircraft (KA-6)

Photo and Drawing: A-6E/TRAM Intruder
Data: A-6E Intruder

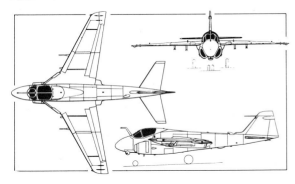

Power plant: Two Pratt & Whitney J52-P-8A turbojet engines (each 9 300 lb; 4 218 kg st)
Wing span: 53 ft 0 in (16.15 m)
Length overall: 54 ft 9 in (16.69 m)
Max T-O weight: 60 400 lb (27 397 kg)
Max level speed at S/L: 562 knots (647 mph; 1 041 km/h)
Max rate of climb at S/L: 9 400 ft (2 865 m)/min

Service ceiling: 47 300 ft (14 415 m)
Combat range with max external stores load: 794 nm (914 miles; 1 471 km)
Armament: Five weapon attachment points, one under fuselage and two under each wing for up to 18 000 lb (8 165 kg) of stores. Typical weapon loads are 30 × 500 lb bombs in clusters of six, or three 2 000 lb general-purpose bombs plus two (300 US gallon 1 135 litre) drop-tanks
Variants:
Initial carrier-based attack bomber, no longer operational, was A-6A. Most were converted to later versions. Current variants are as follows:
EA-6A: Retains partial strike capability but equipped primarily to support strike aircraft and ground forces by suppressing enemy electronic activity and obtaining tactical electronic intelligence within a combat area. Carries over 30 different antennae to detect, locate, classify, record and jam enemy radiation
KA-6D: Refuelling tanker; can also be used as control aircraft for air-sea rescue or as day bomber. Converted from A-6A
A-6E: Advanced version with multi-mode radar and IBM computer: entered service 1972. Many built as new; most remaining A-6As also converted to this standard
A-6E/TRAM: Target recognition and attack multi-sensor version, first flown 1974. Undernose IR/laser turret, CAINS inertial navigation, automatic carrier landing capability, and other improvements. Entered service 1979
In service with: US Navy/Marine Corps (EA-6A, KA-6D, A-6E and A-6E/TRAM)

See also Grumman EA-6B Prowler

First flight 1968

GRUMMAN EA-6B PROWLER (USA)

Four-seat carrier- or land-based advanced ECM aircraft

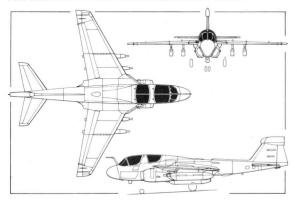

Power plant: Two Pratt & Whitney J52-P-408 turbojet engines (each 11 200 lb; 5 080 kg st)

Wing span: 53 ft 0 in (16.15 m)
Length overall: 59 ft 10 in (18.24 m)
T-O weight: 54 461 lb (24 703 kg) in stand-off jamming configuration; 65 000 lb (29 483 kg) max T-O (catapult or field)
Max level speed at S/L: 533 knots (651 mph; 1 048 km/h) with five ECM pods
Max rate of climb at S/L: 10 030 ft (3 057 m)/min with five ECM pods
Service ceiling: 41 000 ft (12 500 m) with five ECM pods
Range with max external load: 955 nm (1 099 miles; 1 769 km), incl 5% reserves plus 20 min at S/L
Avionics: ALQ-99 advanced electronic countermeasures (ECM) to fulfil tactical electronic warfare role. Five integrally powered pods, with total of 10 jamming transmitters, can be carried. Surveillance receivers in fin-tip pod. First 21 aircraft now upgraded to ICAP (increased capability) standard with more efficient jamming equipment, defensive ECM, automatic carrier landing system, and new nav/com. Prototype flown in 1980 with further-improved (ICAP-2) systems. New APS-130 navigation radar system under development
In service with: US Navy and Marine Corps

Carrier-borne airborne early warning and fighter control aircraft

Photo, Drawing and Data: E-2C Hawkeye

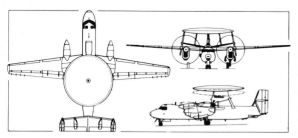

Power plant: Two Allison T56-A-425 turboprop engines (each 4 910 shp)
Wing span: 80 ft 7 in (24.56 m)
Length overall: 57 ft 7 in (17.55 m)
Max T-O weight: 51 900 lb (23 541 kg)

Max level speed: 325 knots (374 mph; 602 km/h)
Service ceiling: 30 800 ft (9 390 m)
Ferry range: 1 394 nm (1 605 miles; 2 583 km)
Time on station, 175 nm (200 miles; 320 km) from base: 4 h
Accommodation: Pilot and co-pilot on flight deck; combat information centre officer, air control officer and radar operator in tactical compartment. Provision for additional operator on long-endurance missions with auxiliary fuel
Avionics: Include APA-171 rotodome (radar and IFF antennae), APS-125 radar processing system with overland/overwater detection capability, IFF interrogator, ALR-59 passive detection system, and air data computer
Variants:
E-2A: Initial production version; full early-warning and command electronics system. Now converted to E-2B
E-2B: Litton Industries L-304 microelectronic general purpose computer. All operational E-2As brought up to this standard
E-2C: Advanced Grumman/General Electric-developed radar capable of detecting airborne targets in a land clutter environment. Improvements for increased reliability and easier maintenance
TE-2C: Training version of E-2C
In service with: Air forces of Israel (E-2C), Japan (E-2C, from 1982), and US Navy (E-2B, E-2C and TE-2C)

Tandem two-seat carrier-borne air superiority and multi-purpose fighter

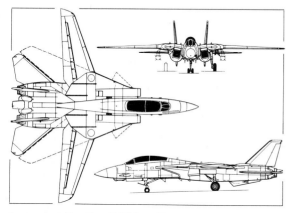

Wing span: spread: 64 ft 1.5 in (19.54 m); swept 38 ft 2.5 in (11.65 m)
Length overall: 61 ft 11.9 in (18.89 m)
Max T-O weight: 74 348 lb (33 724 kg)
Max level speed at height: Mach 2.34 (1 342 knots; 1 545 mph; 2 486 km/h)
Service ceiling: over 50 000 ft (15 250 m)
Range with max internal and external fuel: approx 1 735 nm (2 000 miles; 3 220 km)
Armament: One General Electric M61A1 Vulcan multi-barrel 20 mm gun in port side of forward fuselage. Four Sparrow air-to-air missiles partially submerged under fuselage; or four Phoenix missiles on special pallets attached to underside of fuselage. Two wing pylons, one under each fixed wing section, can carry four Sidewinder missiles, or two additional Sparrow or Phoenix missiles with two Sidewinders. Various combinations of missiles and bombs to a max external weapons load of 14 500 lb (6 577 kg). Grumman-developed 1 760 lb (798 kg) tactical air reconnaissance pod system (TARPS), carried under fuselage, being fitted in 1980-81 to 49 US Navy F-14As. Other operational equipment includes Northrop television camera set (TCS), for automatic target search/acquisition/lock-on, and ALE-39 chaff/flare dispensers with integral jammers. Iranian F-14As retain Phoenix weapon system capability, but have slightly different ECM equipment
In service with: Iranian Air Force and US Navy

Power plant: Two Pratt & Whitney TF30-P-412A turbofan engines (each 20 900 lb; 9 480 kg st with afterburning)

First flight 1959

Side-by-side two-seat observation (OV-1), electronic surveillance (EV-1), armed reconnaissance (JOV-1) and electronic reconnaissance (RV-1) aircraft

Photo and Data: OV-1D Mohawk
Drawing: OV-1A Mohawk

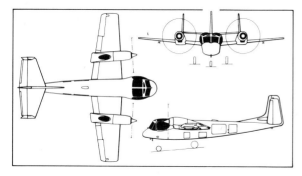

Power plant: Two Avco Lycoming T53-L-701 turboprop engines (each 1 400 shp)
Wing span: 48 ft 0 in (14.63 m)
Length overall: 41 ft 0 in (12.50 m) excl SLAR pod
Max T-O weight: SLAR: 18 109 lb (8 214 kg); IR: 17 912 lb (8 124 kg)

Max level speed at 10 000 ft (3 050 m), 40% fuel: SLAR: 251 knots (289 mph; 465 km/h); IR: 265 knots (305 mph; 491 km/h)
Max rate of climb at S/L: SLAR: 3 466 ft (1 056 m)/min; IR: 3 618 ft (1 102 m)/min
Service ceiling: 25 000 ft (7 620 m)
Max range with external tanks at 20 000 ft (6 100 m): SLAR: 820 nm (944 miles; 1 520 km); IR: 878 nm (1 011 miles; 1 627 km)
Equipment: Photo surveillance system consists of two KA-60C 180-degree panoramic camera systems and one KA-76 serial frame camera. Infra-red AN/AAS-24 surveillance system. Alternative AN/APS-94D side-looking airborne radar (SLAR) system. ECM pods and an LS-59A photoflash unit can be carried on underwing stations.
Variants:
OV-1A: Initial production version with T53-L-3 engines, equipped for day and night reconnaissance; 42 ft (12.80 m) wing span
JOV-1A: OV-1A with provision for 500 lb bombs, FFAR rockets and 0.50 in machine-gun pods on hardpoints
OV-1B: APS-94 side-looking airborne radar, in pod under forward fuselage, and internal camera
EV-1: Conversion of OV-1B to electronic surveillance aircraft with AN/ALQ-133 radar target locator system in underfuselage and wingtip pods
In service with: Israeli Air Force (EV-1) and US Army (OV-1A/B/C/D, JOV-1A, RV-1C/D, and EV-1)
OV-1C: T53-L-3 engines and greater all-up weight. AAS-24 infra-red mapping sensor and internal camera
OV-1D: T53-L-701 engines and increased wing span. Side-looking airborne radar, or infra-red, or other sensors. New cameras
RV-1C/D: OV-1C/Ds modified for electronic reconnaissance

First flight 1952

Four-seat carrier-borne anti-submarine attack aircraft

Photo: CP-121
Drawing and Data: S-2E Tracker

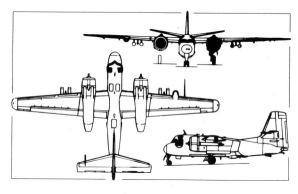

Power plant: Two Wright R-1820-82WA piston engines (each 1 525 hp)
Wing span: 72 ft 7 in (22.13 m)
Length overall: 43 ft 6 in (13.26 m)
Max T-O weight: 29 150 lb (13 222 kg)
Max level speed at S/L: 230 knots (265 mph; 426 km/h)

Service ceiling: 21 000 ft (6 400 m)
Ferry range: 1 128 nm (1 300 miles; 2 095 km)
Armament: Fuselage bay for 60 echo-sounding depth charges. One Mk 101 or Mk 57 nuclear depth bomb or equivalent store in bomb bay. Six underwing pylons for torpedoes, 5 in rockets, etc; 32 sonobuoys in nacelles
Variants:
S-2A: First production version. Wing span 69 ft 8 in (21.25 m), length 42 ft (12.80 m), max T-O weight 26 300 lb (11 929 kg). Canadian version designated *CP-121*
S-2B: Similar to S-2A but with Julie/Jezebel active/passive anti-submarine detection equipment
TS-2B: Trainer version of S-2B
S-2C: Similar to S-2A but with asymmetric bulged bomb bay to house two homing torpedoes. Most converted to US-2C or RS-2C
S-2D: Improved anti-submarine equipment, wider cockpit, and longer range
S-2E: Improved anti-submarine equipment
S-2F: As S-2B but with uprated submarine detection equipment
S-2G: S-2E uprated with Martin Marietta avionics kit
US-2A/C: S-2A/C converted for target towing
US-2B: Utility transport conversion of S-2B
RS-2C: S-2C converted for photo reconnaissance/survey work
AS-2D: S-2D modified for night attack
In service with: Air forces of Argentina (Navy S-2A), Australia (Navy S-2G), Brazil (S-2A/CS2F-1), Canada (CP-121, formerly CS2F-1/2/3), Japan (Navy S-2A), South Korea (S-2F), Peru (Navy S-2E), Taiwan (S-2A), Thailand (S-2A), Turkey (Navy S-2E and TS-2A), Uruguay (S-2A), USA (Navy TS-2A/US-2A, TS-2B/US-2B, US-2C/RS-2C, S-2D, S-2E and S-2G) and Venezuela (Navy S-2E)

Single-seat lightweight fighter and ground attack aircraft; two-seat trainer

Photo, Drawing and Data: Ajeet

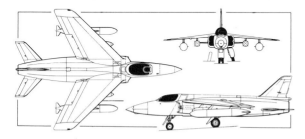

Power plant: One Rolls-Royce Orpheus 701-01 turbojet engine (4 500 lb; 2 041 kg st)
Wing span: 22 ft 1 in (6.73 m)
Length overall: 29 ft 8 in (9.04 m)
T-O weight 'clean': 7 803 lb (3 539 kg)
Max T-O weight: 9 195 lb (4 170 kg)

Max level speed at 39 375 ft (12 000 m): 'clean' aircraft: 550 knots (634 mph; 1 020 km/h)
Max level speed at S/L: 'clean' aircraft: 595 knots (685 mph; 1 102 km/h)
Time to 39 375 ft (12 000 m): 'clean' aircraft: 6 min 2 s
Service ceiling: 45 000 ft (13 720 m)
Combat radius at low level: with two 500 lb bombs: 110 nm (127 miles; 204 km); with four Arrow rocket pods: 104 nm (120 miles; 193 km)
Armament: Two 30 mm Aden Mk 4 cannon in air intake fairings, one on each side of fuselage (each with 90 rds). Four underwing hardpoints able to carry two 500 lb bombs (inner pylons), four Arrow Type 122 pods each containing 18 × 68 mm rockets, or two 150 litre (33 Imp gallon) drop-tanks (outer pylons)
Variants:
Gnat Mk 1: Initial production single-seat fighter version. Licence-built by Hindustan Aeronautics Ltd in India 1962-73. Expected to be phased out of service in 1981
Ajeet: 'Mk 2' single-seat fighter, developed from the Gnat by HAL in India. Integral wing fuel tanks, more advanced equipment
Ajeet Trainer: Tandem two-seat version of Ajeet, with same power plant, reduced fuselage fuel, lengthened fuselage (34 ft 3 in; 10.44 m). Aden guns deleted, but provision for external stores retained. Under development
In service with: Indian Air Force (Gnat Mk 1 and Ajeet)

First flight 1961

Single-seat ground attack fighter (Mk I) and tandem two-seat operational trainer (Mk IT)

Photo, Drawing and Data: HF-24 Marut Mk I

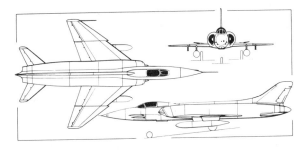

Power plant: Two HAL-built Rolls-Royce Orpheus 703 turbojet engines (each 4 850 lb; 2 200 kg st)

Wing span: 29 ft 6¼ in (9.00 m)
Length overall: 52 ft 0¾ in (15.87 m)
Max T-O weight: early aircraft, without extended-chord wings: 24 085 lb (10 925 kg). Later aircraft, with extended-chord wings: 24 048 lb (10 908 kg)
Max level speed at 39 375 ft (12 000 m): 584 knots (673 mph; 1 083 km/h)
Max permissible speed at S/L: 600 knots (691 mph; 1 112 km/h) IAS
Time to 40 000 ft (12 200 m): 'clean' aircraft: 9 min 20 s
Combat radius (Mk IT): at low level: 129 nm (148 miles; 238 km); interception mission at 39,375 ft (12 000 m): 780 nm (898 miles; 1 445 km)
Armament: Four 30 mm Aden Mk 2 guns in nose (each with 120 rds); retractable pack of 50 SNEB 68 mm air-to-air rockets in lower fuselage aft of nosewheel unit. Attachments for four 1 000 lb bombs, napalm tanks, Type 116 SNEB rocket packs, clusters of T10 air-to-surface rockets, drop-tanks or other stores under wings
Variants:
Mk I: Standard single-seat version, as described
Mk IT: Tandem two-seat operational trainer. As Mk I but without internally-stowed rocket pack
In service with: Indian Air Force (Mks I and IT)

Flight refuelling tanker

Photo, Drawing and Data: Victor K Mk 2 tanker

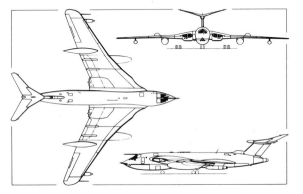

Power plant: Four Rolls-Royce Conway RCo.17 Mk 201 turbofan engines (each 20 600 lb; 9 344 kg st)
Wing span: 117 ft 0 in (35.66 m)
Length overall: 114 ft 11 in (35.03 m)
Max T-O weight: over 170 000 lb (77 110 kg)
Max level speed at 40 000 ft (12 190 m): over 521 knots (600 mph; 965 km/h)
Service ceiling: over 60 000 ft (18 300 m)
Max range: 3 995 nm (4 600 miles; 7 400 km)
Current variant:
K Mk 2: B Mk 2 bombers and SR Mk 2 strategic reconnaissance aircraft converted to tankers, deliveries starting in May 1974. Wing span reduced by 3 ft (0.91 m)
In service with: Royal Air Force

First flight 1951

HAWKER HUNTER (UK)

Single-seat fighter, ground attack and reconnaissance aircraft and side-by-side two-seat trainer

Photo: Hunter FGA Mk 78
Drawing and Data: Hunter FGA Mk 9

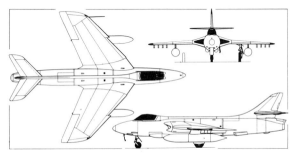

Power plant: One Rolls-Royce Avon Mk 207 turbojet engine (10 000 lb; 4 540 kg st)
Wing span: 33 ft 8 in (10.26 m)
Length overall: 45 ft 10½ in (13.98 m)

Max T-O weight: 24 000 lb (10 885 kg)
Max level speed at S/L: 616 knots (710 mph; 1 142 km/h)
Max rate of climb at S/L: approx 8 000 ft (2 440 m)/min
Service ceiling: 50 000 ft (15 240 m)
Range with external tanks: 1 595 nm (1 840 miles; 2 965 km)
Armament: Four 30 mm Aden cannon in nose (each with 150 rds). On the inboard wing pylons two 1 000 lb bombs, two 500 lb bombs, two clusters of 12 × 3 in rockets, or two packs each containing 37 × 2 in rockets: 24 × 3 in rockets on outboard pylons
Current basic variants:
F Mk 6: Powered by Rolls-Royce Avon 203 turbojet engine. Mks 56 and 58 similar
FGA Mk 9: Ground attack version. Mks 57, 59, 71 and 73 similar
FR Mk 10: Reconnaissance version
GA Mk 11: F Mk 4 converted to ground attack trainer for Royal Navy. Rolls-Royce Avon 122 engine and armed with Bullpup missile
T Mk 7/8/53/62/66/67/69/75/77/80: Two-seat trainers
In service with: Air forces of Abu Dhabi (FGA Mk 76/FR Mk 76A and T Mk 76A), Chile (FGA Mk 71 and T Mk 77), India (FGA Mk 56 and T Mk 66), Iraq (FGA Mk 59, FR Mk 10 and T Mk 69), Lebanon (F Mk 6, FB Mk 9 and T Mk 69), Oman (FGA Mk 73 and T Mk 66B), Qatar (FGA Mk 78), Singapore (FGA Mk 74, FR Mk 74A and T Mk 75), Switzerland (F Mk 58 and T Mk 68), UK (Air Force T Mk 7 and FGA Mk 9; Navy T Mk 8 and GA Mk 11), and Zimbabwe (FGA Mk 9)

First flight 1958

HAWKER SIDDELEY BUCCANEER (UK)

Tandem two-seat carrier-borne and land-based low-level strike aircraft

Photo and Drawing: Buccaneer S Mk 2B
Data: Buccaneer S Mk 2A/2B

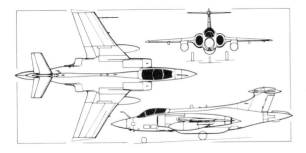

Power plant: Two Rolls-Royce RB 168-1A Spey Mk 101 turbofan engines (each 11 100 lb; 5 035 kg st)
Wing span: 44 ft 0 in (13.41 m)
Length overall: 63 ft 5 in (19.33 m)
Max T-O weight: 62 000 lb (28 123 kg)

Max design level speed at 200 ft (61 m): 560 knots; 1 038 km/h)
Max rate of climb at S/L: approx 7 000 ft (2 135 m)/min
Service ceiling: over 40 000 ft (9 145 m)
Typical strike range: 2 000 nm (2 300 miles; 3 700 km)
Armament: Rotating weapons bay door can carry four 1 000 lb HE Mk 10 bombs, a 440 Imp gallon (2 000 litre) fuel tank, or a reconnaissance pack. Each of the four wing pylon stations can be adapted to carry a wide variety of external stores. Typical loads for any one pylon include one 1 000 lb HE Mk N1 or Mk 10 bomb; two 500 lb or 540 lb bombs on tandem carriers; one 18-tube 68 mm rocket pod; one 36-tube 2 in rocket pod; 3 in rockets; or an HSD/Matra Martel air-to-surface missile. Each pylon is also suitable for carrying three 1 000 lb stores on triple release ejection units, or six 500 lb stores on multiple ejection release units, with only small restrictions on the flight envelope. Max internal and external stores load is 16 000 lb (7 257 kg)
Variants:
S Mk 2A: RAF version without Martel capability
S Mk 2B: RAF version with ability to carry Martel missiles
S Mk 2C: Royal Navy version without Martel capability. Passed on to RAF
S Mk 2D: Royal Navy version with ability to carry Martel missiles. Passed on to RAF
S Mk 50: 'Navalised' (though shore-based) version for South Africa. Basically as original S Mk 2 but with Bristol Siddeley BS.605 rocket motor in rear fuselage (8 000 lb; 3 628 kg st) to boost take-off
In service with: Air forces of South Africa (S Mk 50) and UK (S Mk 2)

First flight 1949

HAWKER SIDDELEY (AVRO) SHACKLETON (UK)

Maritime reconnaissance (MR Mk 3) and airborne early warning (AEW Mk 2) aircraft

Photo: Shackleton MR Mk 3
Drawing and Data: Shackleton AEW Mk 2

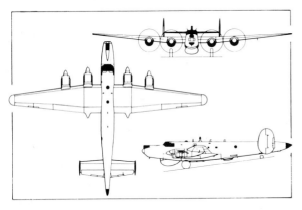

Power plant: Four Rolls-Royce Griffon 57A piston engines (each 2 455 hp)
Wing span: 119 ft 10 in (36.52 m)
Length overall: 87 ft 4 in (26.62 m)
Max level speed: 152 knots (175 mph; 282 km/h)
Range: 2 515 nm (2 900 miles; 4 665 km)
Variants:
AEW Mk 2: Airborne early warning conversion of MR Mk 2; weapons bay modified, retractable 'dustbin' radome deleted, APS-20 search radar in large 'guppy' radome added forward of weapons bay. Various aerials, antennae and equipment fairings along top and bottom of fuselage
MR Mk 3: Development of MR Mk 2, with tricycle landing gear, improved cockpit canopy, dorsal turret deleted, and new outer wing panels incorporating permanent tip-tanks
In service with: Air forces of South Africa (MR Mk 3) and UK (AEW Mk 2)

Medium attack and tactical support bomber; strategic reconnaissance aircraft

Photo, Drawing and Data: Vulcan B Mk 2

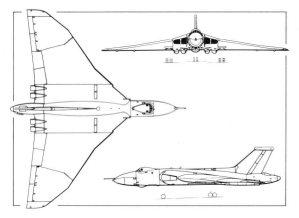

Power plant: Four Rolls-Royce Olympus Mk 301 turbojet engines (each 20 000 lb; 9 072 kg st)
Wing span: 111 ft 0 in (33.83 m)
Length overall: 99 ft 11 in (30.45 m)
Max T-O weight: over 180 000 lb (81 645 kg)
Max cruising speed at 50 000 ft (15 240 m): over 542 knots (625 mph; 1 005 km/h)
Max cruising height: 55 000 ft (16 750 m)
Combat radius: at high and low altitude: 1 500 nm (1 725 miles; 2 780 km). At high altitude: 1 995 nm (2 300 miles; 3 700 km). With flight refuelling: 2 495 nm (2 875 miles; 4 630 km)
Accommodation: Pilot, co-pilot, navigator, air electronics officer and radar operator
Armament: Weapon load can include free-fall nuclear weapons or 21 × 1 000 lb HE bombs
Current variants:
B Mk 2: Major production and service version, with in-flight refuelling capability. Currently serves in overland strike instead of original strategic bombing role
SR Mk 2: Conversion of B Mk 2 for strategic reconnaissance; one squadron in service with RAF
In service with: Royal Air Force (B Mk 2 and SR Mk 2)

First flight 1975

HUGHES AH-64 (USA)

Two-seat twin-engined advanced attack helicopter

Photo and Data: YAH-64

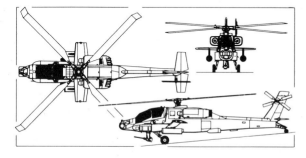

Power plant: Two General Electric T700-GE-700 turboshaft engines (each 1 536 shp)

Main rotor diameter: 48 ft 0 in (14.63 m)
Length overall: 57 ft 9 in (17.60 m), rotors turning
Max T-O weight: 17 650 lb (8 006 kg)
Max level speed: 167 knots (192 mph; 309 km/h)
Max vertical rate of climb at S/L: 2 880 ft (878 m)/min
Service ceiling: 20 500 ft (6 250 m)
Max range, internal fuel: 330 nm (380 miles; 611 km)
Armament: One 30 mm Hughes XM230E1 chain gun, with 1 200 rounds, in underfuselage turret. Four underwing pylons for 16 Hellfire anti-tank guided missiles, 76 × 2.75 in FFAR rockets in four packs, or a mixture of missiles and rockets. FLIR sighting equipment, laser ranger/target designator and laser tracker.
Ordered for: US Army. Selected in 1976 after competitive evaluation against Bell's YAH-63 to meet US Army's AAH (Advanced Attack Helicopter) requirement. Two flight test prototypes followed by three armament/avionics development aircraft plus three more as 'total systems aircraft'. Design modifications since first flight have included swept main rotor blade tips, Hughes 'Black Hole' engine infra-red suppression, and single-curvature cockpit side panels. End of 56-month development programme, and announcement of production decision, are due in 1981. Entry into service is anticipated for 1984; US Army's stated requirement is for 536 aircraft

First flight 1968

Multi-purpose military light helicopter

Photo and Drawing: Model 500MD/TOW

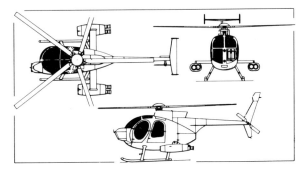

Power plant: One Allison 250-C20B turboshaft engine (420 shp)
Diameter of main rotor: 26 ft 6 in (8.08 m)
Length overall: 30 ft 6 in (9.30 m), rotors fore and aft
Max T-O weight: 500MD/ASW: 3 550 lb (1 610 kg)
Typical ASW mission radius: 22-87 nm (25-100 miles; 40-160 km)
Typical time on station: 500MD/ASW: 1 h 48 min
Armament and operational equipment: Alternative weapons for Standard Scout include 14 × 2.75 in rockets, a 7.62 mm Minigun

HUGHES MODEL 500MD DEFENDER (USA)

(with 2 000 rds), a 40 mm grenade launcher, a 7.62 mm chain gun (with 2 000 rds), or a 30 mm chain gun (with 600 rds). Missile installation of 500MD/TOW comprises four pod-mounted TOW anti-tank missiles, two each side on a tubular mount carried through lower aft fuselage. Martin Marietta mast-mounted sight and laser rangefinder/target designator on Quiet Advanced Scout. Model 500MD/ASW has search radar in nose 'thimble', towed MAD, and two Mk 44 or Mk 46 homing torpedoes; Defender II can have Hughes 30 mm chain gun, a pod containing two Stinger air-to-air missiles, and radar warning system

Variants:
Model 500MD Standard Scout: Basic military version
Model 500MD/TOW: Anti-tank version
Model 500MD Quiet Advanced Scout: Similar to Standard Scout, but with slower-turning four-blade tail rotor and Martin Marietta mast-mounted sight with laser rangefinder/designator
Model 500MD/ASW: Anti-submarine and surface search version, capable of locating enemy destroyers and gunboats up to 150 nm (172 miles; 275 km) from its ship-base during a 2 h patrol
Model 500MD Defender II: Multi-mission version with five-blade main rotor as standard, four-blade tail rotor optional. Other options (see also under 'Armament' above) include Hughes 'Black Hole' infra-red suppression system, pilot's night vision sensor, and advanced avionics/mission equipment package
In service with: Air forces of Argentina, Denmark (Army), Israel (500MD/TOW), Kenya (Army, 500MD and 500MD/TOW), South Korea (500MD and 500MD/TOW), Morocco, Spain (Navy, 500MD/ASW), and Taiwan (Navy, 500MD/ASW)

First flight 1973

IAI KFIR (LION CUB) and NESHER (EAGLE) (Israel)

Single-seat interceptor and close support aircraft; two-seat trainer

Photo, Drawing and Data: Kfir-C2

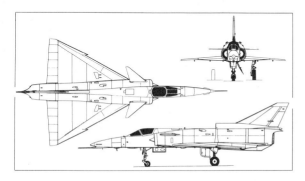

Power plant: One General Electric J79-J1E turbojet engine (17 860 lb; 8 101 kg st with afterburning)

Wing span: 26 ft 11½ in (8.22 m)

Length overall: 51 ft 4¼ in (15.65 m) incl nose probe

Max combat T-O weight: 32 408 lb (14 700 kg)

Max level speed above 36 000 ft (11 000 m): over Mach 2.3 (1 320 knots; 1 520 mph; 2 446 km/h)

Max level speed at S/L: 'clean': 750 knots (863 mph; 1 389 km/h)

Stabilised ceiling (combat configuration): 58 000 ft (17 680 m)

Combat radius, 20 min fuel reserves: interceptor with two Shafrirs and two drop-tanks: 187 nm (215 miles; 346 km); combat air patrol with two Shafrirs and three drop-tanks, incl 1 h patrol: 377 nm (434 miles; 699 km); ground attack, hi-lo-hi, with two Shafrirs, seven 500 lb bombs and two drop-tanks: 415 nm (477 miles; 768 km)

Armament: Two 30 mm DEFA 552 cannon in undersides of engine air intake trunks (each with 140 rds). Three hardpoints under fuselage and two under each wing for up to 9 468 lb (4 295 kg) of external stores; inboard underwing stations can carry triple ejector racks. One IR homing Rafael Shafrir 2 or AIM-9 Sidewinder air-to-air missile under each outer wing for interception. Typical ground attack loads include 1 × 3 000 lb M118, 2 × 2 000 lb Mk 84, 7 × 980 lb Mk 83, 8 × 820 lb M117, or 11 × 500 lb Mk 82 bombs; 6 × 500 lb 'concrete dibber' bombs; 8 × CBU-24 or -49 cluster bombs; one Rafael Luz-1, Shrike, Maverick or Hobos air-to-surface missile; 8 × 66 Imp gallon (300 litre) napalm containers; four LAU-3/A or -10/A, or two LAU-32/A rocket launchers; five SUU-25C/A flare pods; ECM pods; combinations of 110 or 286 Imp gallon (500 or 1 300 litre) drop-tanks

Variants:

Nesher (Eagle): Initial Israeli adaptation of original Dassault Mirage design, with IAI-built airframe similar to Mirage III/5, fitted with Atar 9C engine and Israeli avionics and equipment. First flown 1969; used in October 1973 war

Kfir-C1: Initial production version of Kfir, equipping two squadrons of Israeli Air Force. Developed by IAI, based on Mirage 5. Main visual differences include a shorter but larger-diameter rear fuselage, more powerful engine, larger and flatter undersurface to front fuselage, large dorsal airscoop forward of tail-fin, longer-stroke

(cont on page 125)

ILYUSHIN Il-18 (USSR)

NATO Reporting Name *Coot-A*
ECM or electronic intelligence aircraft, based on airframe of Il-18 airliner

Power plant: Four Ivchenko AI-20M turboprop engines (each 4 250 ehp)
Wing span: 122 ft 8½ in (37.40 m)
Length overall: 117 ft 9 in (35.90 m)
Max T-O weight: approx 140 000 lb (63 500 kg)
Max cruising speed: about 350 knots (400 mph; 650 km/h)
Equipment: Believed to carry side-looking radar in underbelly pod, which is 33 ft 7½ in (10.25 m) long and 3 ft 9 in (1.15 m) deep. Another container, about 14 ft 5 in (4.4 m) long, on each side of the front fuselage, contains a door over a camera or other sensor. Numerous other antennae are visible
In service with: Soviet Navy

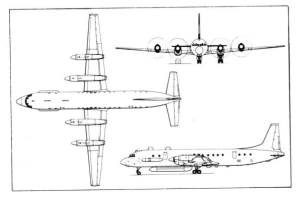

IAI Kfir *(cont from page 123)*

landing gear oleos, and modified wing leading-edges. Israeli navigation and weapon delivery systems, head-up display, gunsight and other equipment
Kfir-C2: Major version, with fixed canard surfaces at front of air intake trunks to improve take-off and landing performance, and to enhance dogfighting capability. Other changes include small strake on each side of nose, and extended leading-edge chord on outer 40% of each wing. Earlier Kfirs being modified to C2 standard
Kfir TC-2: Generally similar to Kfir-C2, but with two seats in tandem under continuous canopy, and very long, drooping nose
In service with: Air forces of Argentina (Nesher, known in Argentina as *Dagger*) and Israel (Kfir-C1 and -C2)

125

First flight 1948

NATO Reporting Names *Beagle* (Il-28) and *Mascot* (Il-28U)
Three-seat tactical bomber, reconnaissance, torpedo bomber and
ECM aircraft; some also converted for target towing and weather
reconnaissance

Photo, Drawing and Data: Il-28

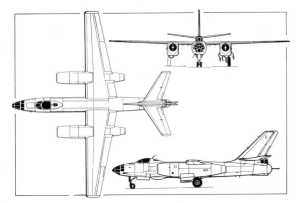

Power plant: Two Klimov VK-1A turbojet engines (each 5 952 lb;
2 700 kg st)
Wing span: 70 ft 4½ in (21.45 m)
Length of fuselage: 57 ft 11 in (17.65 m)
Max T-O weight: 46 738 lb (21 200 kg)

ILYUSHIN Il-28 and HARBIN B-5 (USSR/China)

Max level speed at 14 765 ft (4 500 m): 487 knots (560 mph; 902
km/h)
Time to 32 800 ft (10 000 m): 18 min
Service ceiling: 40 350 ft (12 300 m)
Range with max fuel: 1 295 nm (1 490 miles; 2 400 km)
Armament: Two 23 mm NR-23 cannon (each with 100 rds) in lower
part of nose. Two similar guns (each with 225 rds) on movable
mounting in tail turret. Internal weapons bay for normal and max
loads of 2 205 and 6 614 lb (1 000 and 3 000 kg) respectively. Typi-
cal loads include 4 × 500 kg or 8 × 250 kg bombs; or (Il-28T) one
large or two smaller torpedoes, mines or depth charges. Some
Chinese-built B-5s may carry nuclear bombs. Three to five
cameras, plus 12-18 flares or photoflash bombs, in weapons bay of
Il-28R; provision for single vertical camera in standard Il-28
Variants:
Il-28: Standard version: three-seat tactical light bomber
Il-28U: Two-seat operational/pilot training version, with 'stepped'
additional cockpit forward of pilot's cockpit, 'solid' nose, and
armament and ventral ground-mapping radome deleted
Il-28R: Three-seat tactical reconnaissance version. Tip-tanks stan-
dard; camera or electronic sensor packs in weapons bay; some
have second underfuselage radome
Il-28T: Three-seat torpedo bomber; modified avionics
B-228: Designation of Czechoslovak-built versions
Harbin B-5: Western designation of Chinese-built versions;
Chinese designation H-5
In service with: *Il-28:* Air forces of Afghanistan, Algeria, Egypt,
Hungary, North Korea, Poland, Romania, Somalia, South Yemen,
Syria, USSR, Viet-Nam and Yemen Arab Republic. *B-5:* Albania
and China

First flight about 1971

ILYUSHIN Il-38 (USSR)

NATO Reporting Name *May*

Anti-submarine and maritime patrol aircraft. Based on airframe of Il-18 transport, with lengthened fuselage, fewer cabin windows, and wings mounted further forward to offset CG changes

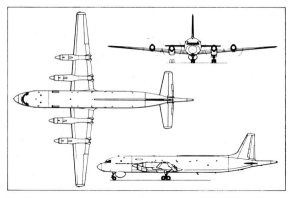

Power plant: Four Ivchenko AI-20M turboprop engines (each 4 250 ehp)

Wing span: 122 ft 8½ in (37.40 m)

Length overall: 129 ft 10 in (39.60 m)

Max T-O weight: approx 140 000 lb (63 500 kg)

Max cruising speed at 27 000 ft (8 230 m): approx 347 knots (400 mph; 645 km/h)

Max range: approx 3 910 nm (4 500 miles; 7 240 km)

Accommodation: Reportedly 12 persons (flight crew plus systems operators)

Equipment: Undernose radome, MAD tail 'sting', other specialised avionics and equipment, and a weapon-carrying capability

In service with: Soviet Navy, Indian Navy

Anti-submarine and anti-ship missile defence helicopter

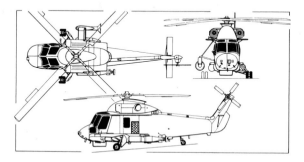

Power plant: Two General Electric T58-GE-8F turboshaft engines (each 1 350 shp)
Main rotor diameter: 44 ft 0 in (13.41 m)
Length overall: 52 ft 7 in (16.03 m), rotors turning
Normal T-O weight: 12 800 lb (5 805 kg)

Max level speed at S/L: 143 knots (165 mph; 265 km/h)
Max rate of climb at S/L: 2 440 ft (744 m)/min
Service ceiling: 22 500 ft (6 860 m)
Normal range with max fuel: 367 nm (422 miles: 679 km)
Accommodation: Pilot, co-pilot and sensor operator. One passenger or litter with LAMPS equipment installed; four passengers or two litters with sonobuoy launcher removed. Provision for carrying internal or external cargo
Armament and equipment: Hard mounts for Mk 46 homing torpedoes. LN 66HP surveillance radar, DIFAR and DICASS acoustic detection/analysis systems, magnetic anomaly detector, associated electronic monitors and controls, smoke markers and flares. External cargo hook, capacity 4 000 lb (1 814 kg); rescue hoist, capacity 600 lb (272 kg)
Current variants:
SH-2D: First major LAMPS (Light Airborne Multi-Purpose System) version, produced by modifying and upgrading earlier models. LN 66 radar, ASQ-81 MAD, AN/SSQ-41 or -47 sonobuoys, Mk 44 or Mk 46 homing torpedoes. All being updated to SH-2F
SH-2F: Current LAMPS version, to which all in-service Seasprites have been or will be updated by 1982
In service with: US Navy

NATO Reporting Name *Hormone*
Anti-submarine search and strike helicopter

Photo, Drawing and Data: *Hormone-A*

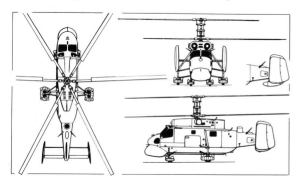

Power plant: Two Glushenkov GTD-3 turboshaft engines (each 900 shp)
Rotor diameter (each): 51 ft 8 in (15.74 m)
Length of fuselage: 32 ft 0 in (9.75 m)
Max T-O weight: approx 16 500 lb (7 500 kg)
Max level speed: 113 knots (130 mph; 209 km/h)
Service ceiling: 11 500 ft (3 500 m)
Range with max fuel, with reserves: 351 nm (405 miles; 650 km)

Accommodation: Pilot, co-pilot, and two or three ASW systems operators. Cabin large enough to contain 12 folding seats for passengers
Armament and equipment: External rack for small stores on each side of the fuselage. Doors under the fuselage of most aircraft enclose a weapon bay for ASW torpedoes and other stores. Some aircraft are believed to carry 'fire and forget' air-to-surface missiles. Dipping sonar housed in compartment at rear of main cabin, immediately forward of tailboom, and search radar under nose of anti-submarine version, which carries also a towed MAD. Some aircraft have a blister fairing over equipment mounted at the base of the centre tail-fin; others have a cylindrical housing, with a transparent top, above the central point of the tailboom, with shallow blister fairing to the rear of this
Variants:
Hormone-A: Basic ship-based ASW version, as described. Believed to lack night/allweather sonar-dipping capability
Hormone-B: Special electronics variant, operated from naval vessels to acquire targets for ship-launched missiles. Larger undernose radome with more spherical undersurface, cylindrical radome under rear of cabin, and data link equipment.
Other versions include a utility model, generally similar to 'Hormone-A' but with unnecessary operational equipment and weapons removed. This version sometimes has a yagi aerial mounted on the nose; it has been photographed in non-operational red and white paint finish. Naval 'Hormones' have been seen carrying an external weapons pod housing long wire-guided torpedoes
In service with: Soviet Navy; air forces of India, Syria and Yugoslavia

Anti-submarine and maritime patrol aircraft, developed from Lockheed P-2 Neptune (which see)

Photo, drawing and data: P-2J

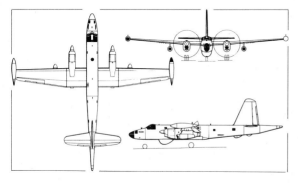

Power plant: Two General Electric T64-IHI-1OE turboprop engines (each 3 060 ehp). Outboard of these, on underwing pylons, are two pod-mounted Ishikawajima J3-IHI-7D turbojets (each 3 417 lb; 1 550 kg st)

Wing span: 97 ft 8½ in (29.78 m)
Length overall: 95 ft 10¾ in (29.23 m)
Max T-O weight: 75 000 lb (34 020 kg)
Max cruising speed: 217 knots (250 mph; 402 km/h)
Max rate of climb at S/L: 1 800 ft (550 m)/min
Service ceiling: 30 000 ft (9 150 m)
Range with max fuel: 2 400 nm (2 765 miles; 4 450 km)
Accommodation: Flight crew of two, plus ten systems and equipment operators in cabin
Operational equipment: Includes AN/APN-187B-N Doppler radar, AN/APS-80-N search radar, HLR-101 electronic support measures, HSQ-101 MAD, AN/ASA-20B Julie recorder, AN/AQA-5-N Jezebel recorder, HQA-101 active sonobuoy indicator, AN/ARR-52A(V) sonobuoy receiver, N-R-86 on-top position indicator, IFF, SIF, Loran, Tacan, and HSA-116 integrated data display system and digital data processor. Searchlight in starboard wingtip pod
Variants:
P-2J: Standard version, as described
UP-2J: Converted P-2J with equipment for ECM and target towing
In service with: Japan (Navy)

Single-seat all-weather tactical strike and reconnaissance fighter

Photo: F-104J Starfighter
Drawing: F-104G Starfighter
Data: F-104S Starfighter

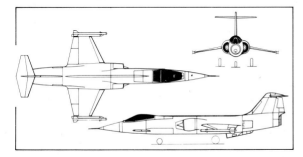

Power plant: One General Electric J79-GE-19 turbojet engine (17 900 lb; 8 120 kg st with afterburning)
Wing span: 21 ft 11 in (6.68 m) without tip-tanks
Length overall: 54 ft 9 in (16.69 m)
Max T-O weight: 31 000 lb (14 060 kg)
Max level speed at 36 000 ft (11 000 m): Mach 2.2 (1 260 knots; 1 450 mph; 2 330 km/h)
Max rate of climb at S/L: 55 000 ft (16 765 m)/min
Service ceiling: 58 000 ft (17 680 m)
Radius with max fuel: 673 nm (775 miles; 1 247 km)

Ferry range, no flight refuelling: 1 576 nm (1 815 miles; 2 920 km)
Armament: Nine external attachment points, at wingtips, under wings and under fuselage, for up to 7 500 lb (3 402 kg) of bombs, rocket pods, auxiliary fuel tanks and air-to-air missiles. Normal primary armament of two AIM-7 Sparrow air-to-air missiles and/or two Sidewinders under fuselage, plus either a Sidewinder or a 170 US gallon (645 litre) fuel tank on each wingtip. Alternatively, an M61 20 mm multi-barrel rotary cannon can be fitted in port underside of fuselage instead of AIM-7 control package
Variants (principal models in current use):
CF-104: Canadian-built equivalent of F-104G
CF-104D: Lockheed-built tandem two-seat trainer for CF-104
F-104G: Single-seat multi-role version; principal model currently in service. Compared with earlier models, has strengthened airframe, upward ejection seat, larger vertical tail surfaces. J79-GE-11A turbojet (15 800 lb; 7 167 kg st with afterburning)
RF-104G: Single-seat reconnaissance/fighter version of F-104G
TF-104G: Tandem two-seat operational trainer version of F-104G
F-104J: Japanese version of F-104G, mostly licence-built by Mitsubishi
F-104S: Final production version, built by Aeritalia for Italian and Turkish air forces. Development of F-104G with uprated J79 engine and Sparrow armament
In service with: Air forces of Belgium (F-104G), Canada (CF-104 and CF-104D), Denmark (F-104G and TF-104G), German Federal Republic (Air Force F-104G and TF-104G; Navy F-104G, RF-104G and TF-104G), Greece (F-104G), Italy (F-104G, F-104S and TF-104G), Japan (F-104J and F-104DJ), Netherlands (F-104G, RF-104G and TF-104G), Norway (F-104G and TF-104G), Taiwan (F-104G, RF-104G and TF-104G), and Turkey (F-104G, F-104S and TF-104G)

First flight 1945

LOCKHEED P-2 NEPTUNE (USA)

Maritime patrol bomber

Photo, Drawing and Data: P-2H Neptune

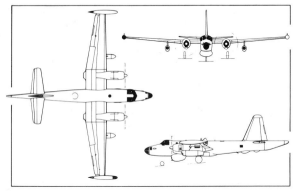

Power plant: Two Wright R-3350-32W piston engines (each 3 500 hp) and two Westinghouse J34 turbojet engines (each 3 400 lb; 1 540 kg st)

Wing span over tip-tanks: 103 ft 10 in (31.65 m)
Length overall: 91 ft 8 in (27.94 m)
Max T-O weight: 79 895 lb (36 240 kg)
Max level speed: 350 knots (403 mph; 648 km/h)
Max level speed at 10 000 ft (3 050 m): 309 knots (356 mph; 573 km/h) with piston engines only
Service ceiling: 22 000 ft (6 700 m)
Max range with ferry tanks: 3 200 nm (3 685 miles; 5 930 km)
Accommodation: Pilot, co-pilot, navigator/bombardier, and four systems/equipment operators
Armament: Provision for sixteen 5 in rocket projectiles under wings. Weapon load of 8 000 lb (3 630 kg), carried internally, may consist of bombs, depth charges or torpedoes. MAD gear and sonobuoy installation. Provision for optional dorsal turret with two 0.50 in machine-guns
Current variants:
P-2H: First version to introduce auxiliary underwing turbojets; other equipment and detail changes
SP-2H: As P-2H, with modernised equipment
In service with: Air forces of Argentina (Navy, P-2H), France (Navy, P-2H), Japan (Navy, P-2H*), Netherlands (Navy, SP-2H) and USA (Navy, SP-2H)

*See also Kawasaki P-2J

Anti-submarine reconnaissance aircraft
Photo and Data: P-3C Orion
Drawing: CP-140 Aurora

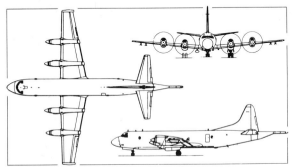

Power plant: Four Allison T56-A-14 turboprops (each 4 910 ehp)
Wing span: 99 ft 8 in (30.37 m)
Length overall: 116 ft 10 in (35.61 m)
Max permissible weight: 142 000 lb (64 410 kg)
Max level speed at 15 000 ft (4 570 m): at AUW of 105,000 lb (47 625 kg): 411 knots (473 mph; 761 km/h)
Mission radius, 3 h on station: 1 346 nm (1 550 miles; 2 494 km)
Armament: Bomb bay can accommodate a 2 000 lb Mk 25/39/55/56 mine, three 1 000 lb Mk 36/52 mines, three Mk 57 depth charges, eight Mk 54 depth bombs, eight Mk 43/44/46 torpedoes or a combination of two Mk 101 nuclear depth bombs and four Mk 43/44/46

torpedoes. Ten underwing pylons for stores. Max total weapon load includes six 2 000 lb mines under wings and a 7 252 lb (3 290 kg) internal load made up of two Mk 101 depth bombs, four Mk 44 torpedoes, sonobuoys, marine markers, BT buoys and flares
Accommodation: Normal crew of ten, including systems/equipment operators
Current operational variants:
WP-3A: Weather reconnaissance version of P-3A; modified radome
P-3B: Follow-on production version. Those of USN modified to carry Bullpup missiles; some converted to EP-3B for ECM duties
P-3C: Advanced version with A-NEW sensors and control equipment. From January 1975, all USN and RAAF P-3Cs fitted with Update I avionics, including Omega navigation, IR detection, and sonobuoy reference systems
RP-3D: Single aircraft for US Naval Oceanographic Office, equipped to map Earth's magnetic field. ASW equipment deleted, extra fuel tanks in weapons bay
WP-3D: Atmospheric research and weather modification experiment version; two modified for US National Oceanic and Atmospheric Administration
EP-3E: ECM version, converted from P-3A and EP-3B; large canoe-shaped radars above and below fuselage, and ventral radome forward of wing
P-3F: Long-range maritime patrol version for Iran
CP-140 Aurora: 18 ordered for Canadian Armed Forces; deliveries began 1980. Basically an Orion with avionics and data processing capability of S-3A Viking
In service with: *Orion:* Air forces of Australia, Iran, Japan (Navy, delivery in 1980s), Netherlands (Navy, from 1981), New Zealand, Norway, Spain and USA (Navy). *Aurora:* Canadian Armed Forces

First flight 1972

LOCKHEED S-3A VIKING (USA)

Carrier-borne anti-submarine aircraft

Photo, Drawing and Data: S-3A Viking

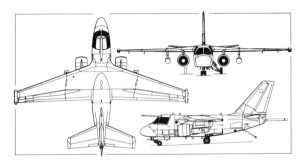

Power plant: Two General Electric TF34-GE-2 turbofan engines (each 9 275 lb; 4 207 kg st)
Wing span: 68 ft 8 in (20.93 m)
Length overall: 53 ft 4 in (16.26 m)
Normal ASW T-O weight: 42 500 lb (19 277 kg)

Max level speed: 450 knots (518 mph; 834 km/h)
Max rate of climb at S/L: over 4 200 ft (1 280 m)/min
Service ceiling: above 35 000 ft (10 670 m)
Combat range: more than 2 000 nm (2 303 miles; 3 705 km)
Ferry range: more than 3 000 nm (3 454 miles; 5 558 km)
Accommodation: Pilot, co-pilot, tactical operator and sensor operator
Armament: Split weapons bays equipped with BRU-14/A bomb rack assemblies can deploy four Mk 36 destructors, four Mk 46 torpedoes, four Mk 82 bombs, two Mk 57 or four Mk 54 depth bombs, or four Mk 53 mines, BRU-11/A bomb racks installed on the two wing pylons permit carriage of SUU-44/A flare launchers, Mk 52, Mk 55 or Mk 56 mines, Mk 20-2 cluster bombs, Aero 1D auxiliary fuel tanks, or two rocket pods on LAU-68/A (7 FFAR 2.75 in), LAU-61/A (19 FFAR 2.75 in), LAU-69/A (19 FFAR 2.75 in), or LAU-10A/A (4 FFAR 5.0 in) launchers. Alternatively, installation of TER-7 triple ejector racks on the BRU-11/A bomb racks makes it possible to carry three rocket pods, flare launchers, Mk 20 cluster bombs, Mk 82 bombs, Mk 36 destructors, or Mk 76-5 or Mk 106-4 practice bombs under each wing
Variants:
S-3A: Standard anti-submarine version, as described
US-3A: Prototype carrier on-board delivery (COD) transport version, first flown in 1976. ASW equipment deleted
In service with: US Navy (S-3A)

Tandem two-seat long-range strategic reconnaissance aircraft

Photo and Drawing: SR-71A
Data: SR-71A; weight and performance estimated

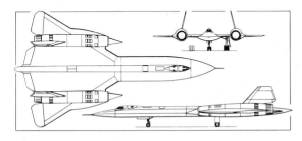

Power plant: Two Pratt & Whitney JT11D-20B (J58) bypass turbojet (turbo-ramjet) engines (each 32 500 lb; 14 740 kg st with afterburning)
Wing span: 55 ft 7 in (16.95 m)
Length overall: 107 ft 5 in (32.74 m)
Max T-O weight: 170 000 lb (77 110 kg)

Max level speed, short periods only: Mach 3.5 (2 005 knots; 2 310 mph; 3 717 km/h)
Max speed, long-range cruising: Mach 3 (1 720 knots; 1 980 mph; 3 186 km/h)
Operational ceiling: over 80 000 ft (24 400 m)
Unrefuelled range, at Mach 3.0 at 78 750 ft (24 000 m): 2 590 nm (2 980 miles: 4 800 km)
Max endurance, unrefuelled, at Mach 3.0 at 78 750 ft (24 000 m): 1 h 30 min
Equipment: Internal equipment ranges from simple battlefield surveillance systems to multiple-sensor high-performance systems for interdiction reconnaissance, and strategic systems capable of specialised surveillance of up to 10 000 sq miles (259 000 km²) of territory in one hour. Photographic, infra-red and electronic sensors housed in forward portions of wing/body chine fairings
Variants:
SR-71A: Strategic photographic and electronic reconnaissance version
SR-71B: Tandem two-seat operational training version, with stepped second cockpit and fixed fins under engine nacelles. Only two examples known, of which one destroyed
SR-71C: Training version, converted from SR-71A to replace one SR-71B lost in crash. Externally similar to SR-71B
In service with: US Air Force

Single-seat high-altitude strategic (U-2) and tactical (TR-1) reconnaissance aircraft

Photo: U-2R
Drawing: U-2R
Data: (A) U-2R; (B) TR-1A

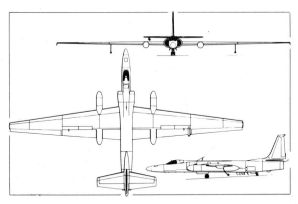

Power plant: (A, B) One Pratt & Whitney J75-P-13 turbojet engine (17 000 lb; 7 711 kg st)
Wing span: (A, B) 103 ft 0 in (31.39 m)
Length overall: (A, B) 63 ft 0 in (19.20 m)
Max T-O weight: (A) 29 000 lb (13 154 kg)
Max level speed at 60 000 ft (18 290 m): (B) approx 373 knots (430 mph; 692 km/h)
Operational ceiling: (B) approx 90 000 ft (27 430 m)
Max range: (B) over 2 605 nm (3 000 miles; 4 830 km)
Max endurance: (A, B) 12 h
Avionics and operational equipment: Up to five 70 mm cameras (A) or UPD-X side-looking airborne radar and ECM (B); other equipment, including PLSS (see below), according to mission
Armament: None
Current variants:
U-2R: Ordered in 1968, primarily to replace losses among earlier models; originally designated WU-2C
TR-1A: Single-seat tactical reconnaissance version, primarily for use in Europe. Selected as airborne relay vehicle for Lockheed PLSS (Precision Location Strike System), intended to locate and identify enemy radar emitters, and to direct strike aircraft against them. First of two prototypes was due to fly in 1981; USAF plans to procure 35
ER-2: Earth resources research aircraft for NASA, modified from TR-1A; one delivered
In service with: US Air Force (U-2)

Tandem two-seat light tactical bomber (B-57B) and defence evaluation aircraft (EB-57B)

Photo: EB-57B
Drawing and data: B-57B

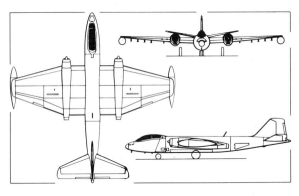

Power plant: Two Wright J65-W-5F turbojet engines (each 7 200 lb; 3 265 kg st)
Wing span: 64 ft 0 in (19.50 m)
Length overall: 65 ft 6 in (19.96 m)
Max T-O weight: 55 000 lb (24 950 kg)
Max speed at 40 000 ft (12 200 m): 505 knots (582 mph; 936 km/h)
Rate of climb at S/L: 3 500 ft (1 066 m)/min
Service ceiling: 48 000 ft (14 630 m)
Range with max fuel: 2 000 nm (2 300 miles; 3 700 km)
Armament: Eight 0.50 in machine-guns in nose. Eight underwing pylons for total of 16 rockets. Rotary bomb-bay for 6 000 lb (2 720 kg) of bombs
Current variants:
B-57B: Intruder bomber developed from British Canberra (which see). Differences include tandem seating for crew, new engines and revised armament and equipment
EB-57B: Conversion of B-57B still used by Air National Guard's 158th Defense System Evaluation Group. Equipped with the latest devices for jamming and penetrating air defences, the task of the EB-57Bs is to simulate an enemy bomber force, and attempt to find gaps in air defence systems by day or night, at variable altitudes and from any point of the compass
In service with: Air forces of Pakistan (B-57B) and USA (EB-57B)

Twin-turbine multi-purpose helicopter

Photo, Drawing and Data: BO 105P (PAH-1)

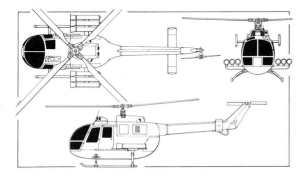

Power plant: Two Allison 250-C20B turboshaft engines (each 420 shp)
Main rotor diameter: 32 ft 3½ in (9.84 m)
Length overall: 38 ft 11 in (11.86 m)
Max T-O weight: 5 291 lb (2 400 kg)

Max cruising speed at 3 280 ft (1 000 m): 113 knots (130 mph; 210 km/h)
Max rate of climb at S/L: 1 375 ft (420 m)/min
Service ceiling: 9 850 ft (3 000 m)
Endurance on PAH-1 missions, with 20 min reserves: 1 h 30 min
Armament: Provision for various military loads, including six Hot anti-tank missiles, mounted on outriggers on each side of fuselage
Variants:
BO 105C: Initial production version, fitted normally with five seats; 400 shp Allison 250-C20 engines
BO 105CB: Standard production from 1975; 420 shp C20B engines. Assembled also by PADC in the Philippines
BO 105D: Version of 105CB for UK, with modified equipment
BO 105CBS: Version with up to six seats in extended cabin
BO 105LS: Uprated version, with 550 shp C28C engines and AUW of 5 512 lb (2 500 kg) with external load
BO 105M (VBH): Liaison/observation version for German Army. Deliveries began 1980 to replace Alouette IIs
BO 105 (PAH-1): Anti-tank version for German Army, with six Hot missiles and stabilised sight. Crew comprises pilot and weapon operator
NBO 105: Version, generally similar to BO 105CB, manufactured by PT Nurtanio in Indonesia. Used by all three Indonesian services
In service with: Air forces of Brunei, German Federal Republic (Army), Indonesia (Army, Navy, Air Force), Lesotho, Malaysia, Netherlands (Army), Nigeria, Philippines (Navy, Air Force), Sierra Leone, Spain (Army) and Sudan

First flight 1954

McDONNELL F-101 VOODOO (USA)

Tandem two-seat long-range interceptor fighter

Photo: CF-101B Voodoo
Drawing and Data: F-101B Voodoo

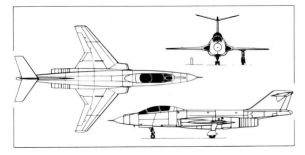

Power plant: Two Pratt & Whitney J57-P-55 turbojet engines (each 14 880 lb; 6 750 kg st with afterburning)
Wing span: 39 ft 8 in (12.09 m)
Length overall: 67 ft 5 in (20.55 m)
Max T-O weight: 46 500 lb (21 090 kg)
Max level speed at 40 000 ft (12 200 m): Mach 1.85 (1 060 knots; 1 220 mph; 1 963 km/h)
Rate of climb at S/L: 14 000 ft (4 270 m)/min
Service ceiling: 52 000 ft (15 850 m)
Range: 1 345 nm (1 550 miles; 2 495 km)
Armament: Two Genie air-to-air missiles under fuselage and three Falcon air-to-air missiles carried internally
Current variants:
F-101B: Tandem two-seat all-weather interceptor; missile-only armament (see data)
CF-101B: As F-101B, for Canada
TF-101B: Dual-control trainer for F-101B
CF-101F: As TF-101B, for Canada
In service with: Air forces of Canada (CF-101B/F) and USA (F-101B/TF-101B)

First flight 1954

McDONNELL DOUGLAS A-4 SKYHAWK (USA)

Single-seat carrier-borne light attack bomber
Photo, Drawing and Data: A-4M Skyhawk II

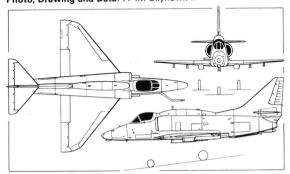

Power plant: One Pratt & Whitney J52-P-408A turbojet engine (11 200 lb; 5 080 kg st)
Wing span: 27 ft 6 in (8.38 m)
Length overall, excl flight refuelling probe: 40 ft 3¼ in (12.27 m)
Max T-O weight: 24 500 lb (11 113 kg)
Max level speed: with 4 000 lb (1 814 kg) bomb load: 560 knots (645 mph; 1 038 km/h)
Ferry range, standard reserves: 1 785 nm (2 055 miles; 3 307 km)
Armament: Provision for several hundred variations of military load, carried externally on one underfuselage rack, capacity 3 500 lb (1 588 kg); two inboard underwing racks, capacity of each 2 250 lb (1 020 kg); and two outboard underwing racks, capacity of each

1 000 lb (450 kg). Weapons that can be deployed include nuclear or HE bombs, air-to-surface and air-to-air rockets, Sidewinder infra-red missiles, Bullpup air-to-surface missiles, ground attack gun pods, torpedoes, countermeasures equipment, etc. Two 20 mm Mk 12 cannon in wing roots standard. DEFA 30 mm cannon available optionally on international versions

Current variants:
A-4F: Single-seat attack bomber; J52-P-8A engine (9 300 lb; 4 218 kg st), avionics in dorsal hump
A-4G: RAN version of A-4F; equipped to carry Sidewinder missiles
A-4H: Version for Israel. Square-topped fin and rudder; two 30 mm DEFA cannon
A-4K: RNZAF version of A-4F; minor differences in equipment
A-4KU: Version for Kuwait. Similar to A-4M
TA-4F/G/H/K: Tandem two-seat trainer versions of A-4F/G/H/K above. Similar *TA-4KU* for Kuwait
TA-4J: Simplified TA-4F for USN, with J52-P-6 or P-8A engine
A-4L: Modified A-4C; uprated engine, improved avionics in hump
A-4M Skyhawk II: Improved A-4F. Square-topped fin and rudder
OA-4M: Forward air control version for USMC, converted from TA-4F. Avionics and weapons capability as for A-4M
A-4N Skyhawk II: Export version of A-4M
A-4P/A-4Q: Updated A-4B for Argentine Air Force/Navy
A-4S: Updated A-4B for Singapore (plus *TA-4S* trainer with stepped cockpits)
A-4Y: Updated A-4M for USMC; new head-up display, redesigned cockpit, Hughes Angle Rate Bombing System
In service with: Air forces of Argentina (Air Force and Navy), Australia (Navy), Indonesia, Israel, Kuwait, Malaysia, New Zealand, Singapore and USA (Navy/Marine Corps)

Tandem two-seat multi-mission land- and carrier-based fighter, fighter-bomber and reconnaissance aircraft
Photo: F-4E Phantom II
Drawing: F-4E Phantom II, with additional side view (top) of FGR Mk 2
Data: F-4EJ Phantom II

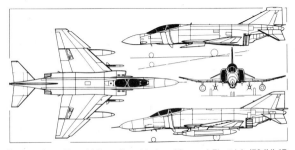

Power plant: Two Ishikawajima-Harima (General Electric) J79-IHI-17 turbojet engines (each 17 900 lb; 8 120 kg st with afterburning
Wing span: 38 ft 5 in (11.71 m)
Length overall: 62 ft 11¾ in (19.20 m)
Max T-O weight: 57 400 lb (26 035 kg)
Max level speed: Mach 2.2 (1 260 knots; 1 450 mph; 2 330 km/h)
Max rate of climb at S/L: 49 500 ft (15 100 m)/min
Service ceiling: 58 050 ft (17 700 m)
Range: 1 600 nm (1 840 miles; 2 960 km)
Armament: Internally mounted M61A1 20 mm multi-barrel gun.

Launchers for Mitsubishi AAM-2 and Sparrow III air-to-air missiles. Five attachments under wings and fuselage for stores
Current variants:
RF-4B: Unarmed reconnaissance version for USMC. J79-GE-8 engines
F-4C: First USAF fighter version. Developed from early USN F-4B with GE-15 engines, different radar and avionics etc
RF-4C: USAF reconnaissance counterpart to F-4C; modified nose
F-4D: F-4C development; same engines, upgraded avionics
F-4E: USAF multi-role fighter; GE-17 engines, slats, more fuel, M61A1 multi-barrel cannon, improved fire control
F-4EJ: Version of F-4E for Japan; as described
RF-4E: Similar to RF-4C but with GE-17 engines, other F-4E features, and different reconnaissance equipment
F-4F: Fighter for Germany, with slats and modified avionics
F-4G: USAF F-4E modified under Wild Weasel programme to suppress hostile early warning and weapon radar systems. M61 gun deleted, APR-38 antennae under nose, on top of fuselage and on fin
F-4J: Interceptor/ground attack development of earlier F-4B for USN/USMC; GE-10 engines, AJB-7 bombing system etc
F-4K: RAF (ex-RN) version *(FG Mk 1)*; developed from F-4B/E. Rolls-Royce Spey Mk 202/3 turbofan engines (each 20 515 lb; 9 306 kg st with afterburning), folding nose, much British equipment
F-4M: RAF version *(FGR Mk 2)*, generally similar to F-4K
F-4N: Updated F-4B for USN
F-4S: Modified F-4J for USN; strengthened structure, slats
In service with: Air forces of Egypt (F-4E), German Federal Republic (RF-4E and F-4F), Greece (F-4E and RF-4E), Iran (F-4D/E and RF-4E), Israel (F-4E and RF-4E), Japan (F-4EJ and RF-4EJ), South Korea (F-4E), Spain (F-4C), Turkey (F-4E and RF-4E), UK and USA

Single-seat air superiority fighter, with secondary attack capability

Photo: F-15 Strike Eagle
Drawing and Data: F-15A Eagle

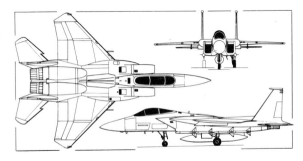

Power plant: Two Pratt & Whitney F100-PW-100 turbofan engines (each approx 25 000 lb; 11 340 kg st with afterburning)
Wing span: 42 ft 9¾ in (13.05 m)
Length overall: 63 ft 9 in (19.43 m)
T-O weight (interceptor): 41 500 lb (18 824 kg)
Max T-O weight: 56 000 lb (25 400 kg)
Max level speed at height: over Mach 2.5 (1 435 knots; 1 650 mph; 2 655 km/h)
Absolute ceiling: 100 000 ft (30 500 m)

Ferry range with FAST Pack auxiliary fuel: over 3 000 nm (3 450 miles; 5 560 km)
Armament: Provision for carriage and launch of a variety of air-to-air weapons over short and medium ranges, including four AIM-9L Sidewinders and four AIM-7F Sparrows. Up to 16 000 lb (7 257 kg) of ordnance or extra ECM equipment on five external hardpoints. One 20 mm M61A1 six-barrel gun
Variants:
F-15A: Initial single-seat fighter version
F-15B: Tandem two-seat operational trainer
F-15C: Development of F-15A, with additional internal fuel, ability to carry FAST Pack conformal fuel/equipment tank against outboard wall of each air intake trunk, and improved avionics. Superseded F-15A in production from 1979
F-15D: Tandem two-seat operational training counterpart of F-15C; superseded F-15B in production
F-15J: Version of F-15C for Japan. Licence production by Mitsubishi
TF-15J: Tandem two-seat operational training counterpart of F-15J for Japan
F-15 Strike Eagle: Prototype all-weather interdictor version of F-15D, built as company-funded demonstrator. Synthetic aperture radar (SAR) for improved target resolution. Crew member in rear seat operates SAR and forward-looking infra-red (FLIR) for navigation and weapons delivery, and monitors enemy tracking systems. External loads can include three 30 mm gun packs or up to 24 000 lb (10 885 kg) of other stores, including anti-radiation and anti-ship missiles
In service with (or ordered by): Air forces of Israel, Japan, Saudi Arabia and USA

McDONNELL DOUGLAS F/A-18 HORNET (USA)

Single-seat carrier-based strike fighter

Photo, Drawing and Data: F/A-18A Hornet

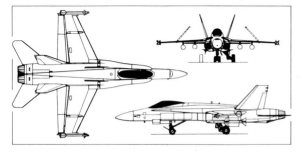

Power plant: Two General Electric F404-GE-400 low bypass turbo-fan engines (each approx 16 000 lb; 7 257 kg st)
Wing span: 37 ft 6 in (11.43 m)
Length overall: 56 ft 0 in (17.07 m)
Max T-O weight: fighter mission, 33 585 lb (15 234 kg); attack mission, 47 000 lb (21 319 kg)
Max level speed: more than Mach 1.8
Combat ceiling: approx 50 000 ft (15 240 m)

Combat radius (internal fuel): fighter mission, over 400 nm (460 miles; 740 km); attack mission, over 550 nm (633 miles; 1 019 km)
Armament: M61 20 mm multi-barrel cannon in nose. Nine weapon stations for up to 17 000 lb (7 710 kg) of external ordnance. Two wingtip stations for Sidewinder air-to-air missiles; two outboard underwing pylons for air-to-ground or air-to-air weapons, including Sparrow missiles; two inboard underwing pylons for air-to-ground weapons or drop-tanks; two nacelle fuselage stations for Sparrows or Martin Marietta AN/ASQ-173 laser spot tracker/strike camera and Ford forward-looking infra-red pods; centreline pylon for external fuel or weapons
Variants:
F/A-18A: Basic single-seat escort fighter/attack aircraft to replace USN F-4, A-4 and A-7. Total of 94 ordered by early 1981; eventual production of 1 388 intended, including 11 development aircraft, TF-18As and 112 reconnaissance models with cameras replacing nose gun. First training squadron commissioned 1980
RF-18A: Tandem two-seat reconnaissance version, with cameras in nose
TFA-18A: Tandem two-seat version of F/A-18A for training, with combat capability. Fuel capacity reduced by under 6 per cent
CF-18A: Version for Canadian Armed Forces, which plan to purchase 137.
F-18L: Multi-role single-seat land-based version for which Northrop is prime contractor. Deletion of naval equipment permits loading of 19 840 lb (9 000 kg) of stores on 11 weapon stations. Two-seat version available
In service with (or ordered by): Canadian Armed Forces (CF-18A) and US Navy (F/A-18A, RF-18A and TF-18A)

McDONNELL DOUGLAS KC-10A EXTENDER (USA)

Flight refuelling tanker/cargo transport

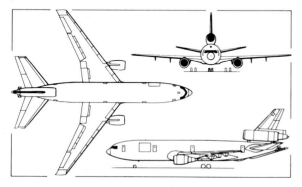

Power plant: Three General Electric CF6-50C2 turbofan engines (each 52 500 lb; 23 815 kg st)
Wing span: 165 ft 4½ in (50.41 m)
Length overall: 181 ft 7 in (55.35 m)
Max T-O weight: 590 000 lb (267 620 kg)
Max cruising speed at 30 000 ft (9 145 m): about 490 knots (564 mph; 908 km/h)
Transfer radius: 1 910 nm (2 200 miles; 3 540 km) with 200 000 lb (90 718 kg) of transfer fuel
Accommodation: Three crew on flight deck. Aerial refuelling station, capable of accommodating boom operator, instructor and student observer, at rear end of lower fuselage compartment. Seats for support personnel at front of main cabin. Cargo door for loading standard pallets, bulk freight or wheeled vehicles in transport role. KC-10A is equipped for both boom and probe and drogue refuelling, and can itself be refuelled in flight
In service with: US Air Force (12 ordered by early 1981)

First flight about 1952   MIKOYAN/GUREVICH MiG-17 (USSR) and SHENYANG F-5 (China)

NATO Reporting Name *Fresco*
Single-seat fighter and ground attack aircraft
Photo, Drawing and Data: MiG-17F

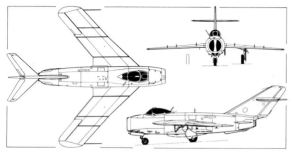

Power plant: One Klimov VK-1F turbojet engine (7 450 lb; 3 380 kg st with afterburning)
Wing span: 31 ft 7 in (9.628 m)
Length overall: 36 ft 11¼ in (11.26 m)
Max T-O weight: 13 393 lb (6 075 kg)
Max level speed at 9 845 ft (3 000 m): 617 knots (711 mph; 1 145 km/h)

Rate of climb at S/L: 12 795 ft (3 900 m)/min
Service ceiling: 54 460 ft (16 600 m)
Max range, with external tanks and bombs: 755 nm (870 miles; 1 400 km)
Armament: One 37 mm N-37D and two 23 mm NR-23 cannon. Provision for four 8-rocket pods or a total of 1 100 lb (500 kg) of bombs beneath the wings
Current variants:
MiG-17F (Fresco-C): Standard day fighter. Built also in Poland as Lim-5 and in Czechoslovakia as S-104
MiG-17PF (Fresco-D): Limited all-weather interceptor. Radar in central bullet in air intake. Otherwise generally same as MiG-17F. Length overall 38 ft 4 in (11.68 m). Max T-O weight 14 000 lb (6 350 kg). Built also in Poland as Lim-5P
Shenyang F-5: Western designation of Chinese-built MiG-17F (Chinese designation *J-5*). Deliveries began late 1956. Also in service with Chinese Air Force, as a standard advanced trainer, is a tandem two-seat variant
Shenyang F-5A: Western designation of Chinese-built MiG-17PF (Chinese designation *J-5jia*)
In service with: MiG-17: Air forces of Afghanistan, Algeria, Angola, Bulgaria, Congo, Cuba, Czechoslovakia, Egypt, Ethiopia, German Democratic Republic, Guinea, Iraq, North Korea, Mali, Mongolia, Nigeria, Poland, Romania, Somalia, South Yemen, Sri Lanka, Syria, Uganda and Yemen Arab Republic. F-5/5A: Albania, China, Sudan, Tanzania, Viet-Nam

NATO Reporting Name *Farmer*
Single-seat fighter and ground attack aircraft

Photo, Drawing and Data: Chinese-built F-6 (MiG-19SF)

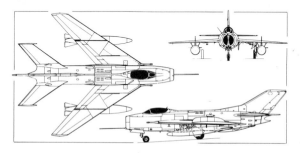

Power plant: Two Shenyang WP-6 (development of Tumansky RD-9BF) turbojet engines (each 7 277 lb; 3 300 kg st with afterburning)
Wing span: 30 ft 2¼ in (9.20 m)
Length overall, excluding probe: 41 ft 4 in (12.60 m)

Max T-O weight: 19 180 lb (8 700 kg)
Max level speed at 32 800 ft (10 000 m): Mach 1.35 (783 knots; 902 mph; 1 452 km/h)
Rate of climb at S/L: 22 638 ft (6 900 m)/min
Service ceiling: 58 725 ft (17 900 m)
Combat radius: 370 nm (425 miles; 685 km)
Armament: Three 30 mm NR-30 cannon. Underwing attachments for two air-to-air missiles, two rockets of up to 212 mm calibre, two packs of eight air-to-air rockets, two 250 kg bombs, drop-tanks or other stores
Variants:
MiG-19SF (Farmer-C): Day fighter-bomber, to which details apply
MiG-19PM (Farmer-D): Limited all-weather fighter, able to carry four *Alkali* missiles. Guns deleted. Radar in bullet in centre of air intake and lip fairing
MiG-19PF (Farmer-D): As MiG-19PM but armed with two wing-root guns and no provision for *Alkali* missiles
F-6: Western designation of all single-seat versions built at Shenyang in China (Chinese designation *J-6*). These include versions of the MiG-19SF and MiG-19PF, and a tactical reconnaissance model with a camera pack in the front fuselage
FT-6: Tandem two-seat training version of F-6
In service with: MiG-19: Air force of Cuba. F-6: Air forces of Albania, Bangladesh, China (and FT-6), Egypt (and FT-6), Kampuchea, Pakistan, Tanzania and Viet-Nam

NATO Reporting Name *Fishbed*
Single-seat day and all-weather fighter
Photo and Data: MiG-21MF
Drawing: MiG-21SMT

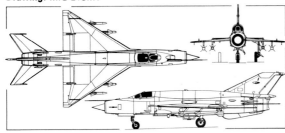

Power plant: One Tumansky R-13-300 turbojet engine (14 550 lb; 6 600 kg st with afterburning)
Wing span: 23 ft 5½ in (7.15 m)
Length, including pitot boom: 51 ft 8½ in (15.76 m)
T-O weight, with four K-13 missiles: 18 078 lb (8 200 kg)
Max level speed: Mach 2.1 (1 203 knots; 1 385 mph; 2 230 km/h)
Design ceiling: 59 050 ft (18 000 m)
Range, internal fuel only: 593 nm (683 miles; 1 100 km)
Armament: Twin-barrel 23 mm GSh-23 gun in lower fuselage. Four underwing pylons for weapons or drop-tanks, including two K-13A *(Atoll)* air-to-air missiles on inner pylons and two *Advanced Atolls* or UV-16-57 packs, each with 16 × 57 mm rockets on outer pylons
Variants:
MiG-21F (Fishbed-C): Short-range clear-weather fighter. R-11 engine. One 30 mm gun and two underwing stores pylons
MiG-21PF (Fishbed-D): Limited all-weather version. Larger R1L radar in intake centrebody. Enlarged air intake. Uprated R-11
Fishbed-E: As MiG-21F. Broader fin. Provision for GSh-23 gun pod
MiG-21FL: Export MiG-21PF with broad fin, uprated R-11 and R2L radar, and provision for gun pod. Built in India
MiG-21PFM (Fishbed-F): Improved MiG-21PF. Further widening of fin. Sideways- (instead of forward-) hinged canopy. R2L radar
MiG-21PFMA (Fishbed-J): Multi-role MiG-21PFM. Deeper dorsal spine fairing. Provision for GSh-23 pod. Four underwing pylons
MiG-21M: As MiG-21PFMA. Built in India
MiG-21R (Fishbed-H): Reconnaissance version of MiG-21PFMA. Pod for cameras, sensors and fuel under belly. Optional wingtip ECM pods. Egyptian version has camera pack recessed in belly
MiG-21MF (Fishbed-J): As MiG-21PFMA, except new R-13 engine
MiG-21RF (Fishbed-H): As MiG-21R but based on MiG-21MF
MiG-21SMT (Fishbed-K): As MiG-21MF, but dorsal spine extended
MiG-21bis (Fishbed-L): Third-generation multi-role version with updated avionics and improved constructional standards
MiG-21bis (Fishbed-N): Advanced Fishbed-L with 16 535 lb (7 500 kg) st Tumansky R-25 turbojet and uprated avionics
MiG-21U (Mongol): Tandem two-seat training versions
F-7: Western designation of versions built at Xian in China (as *J-7*)

In service with: MiG-21: Air forces of Afghanistan, Algeria, Angola, Bangladesh, Bulgaria, Cuba, Czechoslovakia, Egypt, Ethiopia, Finland, German Democratic Republic, Hungary, India, Iraq, North Korea, Laos, Madagascar, Mozambique, Nigeria, Peru, Poland, Romania, Somalia, Sudan, Syria, Uganda, USSR, Viet-Nam, Yemen Arab Republic, South Yemen, Yugoslavia and Zambia. F-7: Albania, China, Egypt and Tanzania

NATO Reporting Name *Flogger-A, B, C, E, F and G*
Variable-geometry air combat fighter
Photo: *Flogger-G*
Drawing and Data: *Flogger-B*

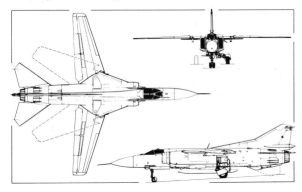

Power plant: One Tumansky R-29B turbojet engine (25 350 lb;
11 500 kg st with afterburning)
Wing span: spread: 46 ft 9 in (14.25 m); swept: 26 ft 9½ in (8.17 m)
Length overall: 55 ft 1½ in (16.80 m)
Max T-O weight: 28 000-33 050 lb (12 700-15 000 kg)
Max level speed: Mach 2.3 (1 320 knots; 1 520 mph; 2 440 km/h)
Service ceiling: 61 000 ft (18 600 m)
Combat radius: 520 nm (600 miles; 960 km)

Armament: Twin-barrel 23 mm GSh-23 gun in belly pack. One
pylon under centre-fuselage, one under each engine air intake
duct, and one under each fixed inboard wing panel for rocket packs,
air-to-air missiles *(Apex* and *Aphid)* or other stores

Operational variants:
MiG-23MF (Flogger-B): Single-seat air combat fighter for Soviet Air
Force, with radar (NATO *High Lark)* in ogival nosecone. Tumansky
R-27 engine in early production models; superseded by current
R-29B. Variable-geometry air intakes and variable nozzle. ECM in
fairings forward of starboard underwing pylon and above rudder.
Undernose laser rangefinder and Doppler. Ventral fin hinged to
fold to starboard, increasing ground clearance, when landing gear
is lowered
MiG-23U (Flogger-C): Two-seat combat/trainer. Identical to early
MiG-23MF except for second cockpit. Tumansky R-27 engine
MiG-23 (Flogger-E): Export version of *Flogger-B.* Smaller radar in
shorter nose radome. No laser rangefinder or Doppler. Armed with
Atoll missiles and GSh-23 gun
MiG-23BM (Flogger-F): Export counterpart of MiG-27 *Flogger-D*
ground attack/interdictor. VG intakes and GSh-23 gun as other
MiG-23s; nose contours, raised seat, cockpit armour and low-
pressure tyres as MiG-27
MiG-23 (Flogger-G): As *Flogger-B,* but much smaller dorsal fin.
New undernose sensor pod
MiG-23BM (Flogger-H): Generally similar to *Flogger-F,* but higher
standard of avionics. Supplied to Warsaw Pact air forces, including
Soviet Air Force
In service with: Air forces of Algeria, Bulgaria, Cuba, Czecho-
slovakia, Egypt, Ethiopia, German Democratic Republic, Hungary,
India, Iraq, Libya, Poland, Syria, USSR and Viet-Nam

NATO Reporting Name *Foxbat*
Single-seat interceptor and reconnaissance aircraft, and two-seat trainer

Photo: *Foxbat-B*
Data: *Foxbat-A*
Drawing: *Foxbat-A,* with additional side view (top) of *Foxbat-C*

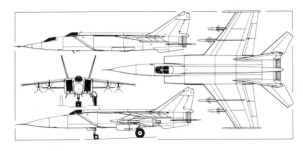

Power plant: Two Tumansky R-31 (R-266) turbojet engines (each 24 250 lb; 11 000 kg st with afterburning)
Wing span: 45 ft 9 in (13.95 m)
Length overall: 78 ft 1¾ in (23.82 m)
Max T-O weight: 79 800 lb (36 200 kg)
Max level speed at height, with missiles: Mach 2.8 (1 605 knots; 1 850 mph; 2 975 km/h)

Service ceiling: 80 000 ft (24 500 m)
Time to 36 000 ft (11 000 m), with afterburning: 2 min 30 s
Normal combat radius: 610 nm (700 miles; 1 130 km)
Armament: Four underwing hardpoints for two *Apex* and two *Aphid,* or four *Acrid,* air-to-air guided weapons
Variants:
MiG-25 (Foxbat-A): Basic single-seat interceptor. As described. Built largely of steel, with titanium wing leading-edges and other parts subjected to extreme heating. Most powerful radar (NATO *Fox Fire*) fitted to any interceptor, but with very little 'lookdown shootdown' capability. High standard of ECCM equipment. Slightly reduced leading-edge sweep towards wingtips
MiG-25R (Foxbat-B): Unarmed reconnaissance version. Five camera windows and flush dielectric panels instead of large radar in nose. Equipment includes side-looking airborne radar. Span 21 in (0.55 m) less than that of *Foxbat-A.* Wing sweep constant. Max speed Mach 3.2 (1 836 knots; 2 115 mph; 3 403 km/h) at height
MiG-25U (Foxbat-C): Trainer. New nose with separate cockpit forward of standard cockpit and lower. No nose radar or reconnaissance equipment
MiG-25R (Foxbat-D): Development of *Foxbat-B.* Larger dielectric nose panel, further aft on starboard side, for side-looking airborne radar. No cameras
E-266M: Designation of experimental version which set world height record of 123,524 ft (37 650 m) in 1977, and time-to-height records. Engines uprated to 30 865 lb (14 000 kg) st. Reported production model with six underwing missiles and large gun. May have 'lookdown shootdown' capability
In service with: Air forces of Algeria, India, Libya, Syria and USSR

NATO Reporting Name *Flogger-D*
Single-seat ground attack fighter

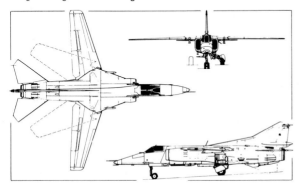

Power plant: One Tumansky R-29B turbojet engine (25 350 lb; 11 500 kg st with afterburning)
Wing span: spread: 46 ft 9 in (14.25 m); swept 26 ft 9½ in (8.17 m)
Length overall: 55 ft 1½ in (16.80 m)
Max T-O weight: 44 310 lb (20 100 kg)

Max level speed at 36 000 ft (11 000 m): Mach 1.75 (1 000 knots; 1 155 mph; 1 860 km/h)
Max speed at S/L: Mach 0.95 (545 knots; 627 mph; 1 010 km/h)
Max ferry range: 1 345 nm (1 550 miles; 2 500 km) with three external tanks
Armament: Five attachments under fuselage and fixed portion of wings for external stores, known to include rocket packs, bombs, tactical nuclear weapons and, probably, AS-7 (NATO *Kerry*) air-to-surface missiles. Bomb rack under each side of rear fuselage. One six-barrel 23 mm gun under fuselage
Variants:
Flogger-D: Completely redesigned forward fuselage compared with MiG-23 interceptor from which it was developed. Nose sharply tapered in side elevation, with small sloping window under a laser rangefinder and marked target seeker at the tip. Raised seat. Additional armour on flat sides of cockpit. Fixed engine air intakes, consistent with primary requirement of high subsonic speed at low altitude. Different gun. Provision for ferry tank under each outer wing, which must be kept in forward position when this is fitted. ECM antenna above port glove pylon. Larger low-pressure tyres
Flogger-F and H: Although these aircraft closely resemble the MiG-27, they are variants of the MiG-23 (which see). They are export versions of the design, but have both served with the Soviet Air Force
In service with: Soviet Air Force

First flight 1961

NATO Reporting Name *Hip*
Medium transport and assault helicopter

Photo, Drawing and Data: *Hip-E* with TV2-117A engines

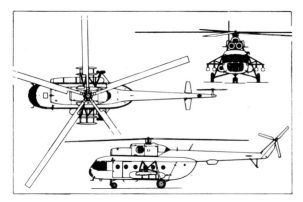

Power plant: Two Isotov TV2-117A turboshaft engines (each 1 700 shp), or (in latest production models) Isotov TV3-117 engines (each 2 200 shp)
Main rotor diameter: 69 ft 10¼ in (21.29 m)
Length of fuselage: 60 ft 0¾ in (18.31 m)
Max T-O weight for VTO: 26 455 lb (12 000 kg)

Max level speed: normal AUW: 140 knots (161 mph; 260 km/h); max AUW 124 knots (142 mph; 230 km/h); with 5 510 lb (2 500 kg) of slung cargo: 97 knots (112 mph; 180 km/h)
Service ceiling: 14 750 ft (4 500 m)
Range: with 28 passengers and 20 min fuel reserves: 270 nm (311 miles; 500 km); with ferry tankage: 647 nm (745 miles; 1 200 km)
Armament: One flexibly-mounted 12.7 mm machine-gun in nose. Triple stores rack on each side of cabin, able to carry up to 192 rockets in six suspended packs, plus four *Swatter* homing anti-tank missiles above racks
Accommodation: Crew of two or three. Up to 32 passengers or 12 stretchers and a medical attendant, or internal/external freight
Variants:
Hip-C: Basic assault transport. Twin-rack for stores on each side of cabin, able to carry a total of 128 57 mm rockets in four packs, or other weapons
Hip-D: As *Hip-C*, but with rectangular-section canisters on outer stores racks and additional antennae. For electronic duties
Hip-E: Described by US Department of Defense as world's most heavily-armed helicopter (see above). Standard equipment of Soviet tactical air forces.
Hip-F: Export counterpart of Hip-E. Missile armament changed to six *Saggers*
In service with: Air forces of Afghanistan, Algeria, Angola, Bangladesh, Bulgaria, China, Cuba, Czechoslovakia, Egypt, Ethiopia, Finland, German Democratic Republic, Guinea-Bissau, Hungary, India, Iraq, Kampuchea, North Korea, Laos, Libya, Madagascar, Mali, Mongolia, Mozambique, Pakistan, Peru, Poland, Romania, Somalia, Sudan, Syria, Uganda, USSR, Viet-Nam, Yemen Arab Republic, South Yemen, Yugoslavia and Zambia

First flight about 1973

NATO Reporting Name *Haze*
Shore-based anti-submarine helicopter

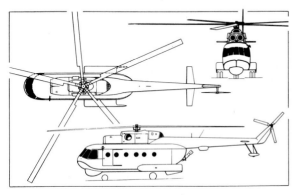

Power plant: Two Isotov TV3-117 turboshaft engines (each 2 200 shp)
Main rotor diameter: 69 ft 10¼ in (21.29 m)
Length overall, rotors turning: 82 ft 9¾ in (25.24 m)
Weights and performance: expected to be generally similar to those of current Mi-8 with TV3-117 engines
Layout and equipment: Derived from the Mi-8, this helicopter is the first known to have been built in the Soviet Union with a boat-hull planing bottom of the kind that has been used successfully for many years on some Sikorsky designs. Combined with a sponson on each side at the rear, this should provide a degree of amphibious capability. The landing gear of the Mi-14 is fully retractable. Equipment includes a large undernose radome and a towed magnetic anomaly detection (MAD) bird stowed against the rear of the fuselage pod
In service with: Bulgarian and Soviet Navies

NATO Reporting Name *Hind-A, B and C*
Armed assault transport helicopter

Photo, Drawing and Data: *Hind-A*

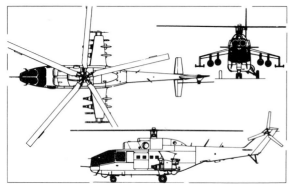

Power plant: Two turboshaft engines generally similar to the Isotov TV2-117A (each 1 500 shp)

Main rotor diameter: approx 55 ft 9 in (17.00 m)
Length of fuselage: approx 55 ft 9 in (17.00 m)
Normal T-O weight: 22 000 lb (10 000 kg)
Armament and accommodation: One 12.7 mm machine-gun under flat bulletproof window in nose. Mountings for four anti-tank guided missiles (NATO *Swatter*) under tips of stub-wings. Four underwing attachments for other stores, including bombs and pods each containing thirty-two 57 mm rockets
Variants:
Hind-A: Initial series production version, with power plant and transmission based on those of Mi-8. Large enclosed flight deck for crew of four; armoured cabin for eight combat-equipped troops. Tail rotor originally on starboard side; transferred to port side retrospectively on operational aircraft. Fully-retractable landing gear
Hind-B: Preceded *Hind-A*. Generally as latter, but stub-wings have neither dihedral nor anhedral and lack the wingtip missile launchers. Limited production only
Hind-C: Development of *Hind-A*, to which it is generally similar except for deletion of nose gun, undernose blister fairing and missile launchers. Tail rotor on port side
Hind-D and E: Gunship versions. Described separately
In service with: Soviet Air Force

NATO Reporting Name *Hind-D and E*
All-weather gunship helicopter

Photo and Drawing: *Hind-D*

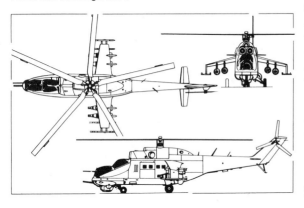

Power plant: Two turboshaft engines generally similar to the Isotov TV2-117A (each 1 500 shp) in original production model. Superseded by Isotov TV3-117 engines (each 2 200 shp) in latest models

Main rotor diameter: approx 55 ft 9 in (17.00 m)
Length of fuselage: approx 55 ft 9 in (17.00 m)
Variants:

Hind-D: This gunship version of the Mi-24 is generally similar to *Hind-C.* The cabin capable of accommodating eight troops is retained but the front fuselage has been completely redesigned forward of the engine air intakes and above the cabin floor structure. There are tandem stations for a weapon operator (in the nose) and pilot, under individual canopies, with the rear seat raised to give the pilot an unobstructed forward view. An unidentified probe, fitted forward of the top starboard corner of the bulletproof windscreen at the extreme nose, may be a sensor to indicate the precise low airspeed conditions when rockets may be fired to ensure minimum dispersion in the rotor downwash. Under the nose is a four-barrel Gatling-type machine-gun in a turret with a wide range of movement in azimuth and elevation. Immediately aft of this is an undernose sensor pack, including probably radar and low light-level TV to enhance capability in bad weather or at night. Launchers for four *Swatter* anti-tank guided missiles under tips of stub-wings. Four underwing attachments for other stores, including bombs and pods each containing thirty-two 57 mm rockets
Hind-E: As *Hind-D,* but with four laser-homing tube-launched anti-tank missiles (NATO *Spiral*) instead of *Swatters,* and structural hardening by substitution of steel and titanium for aluminium in critical components

In service with: *Hind-D:* Air forces of Afghanistan, Algeria, Bulgaria, Czechoslovakia, German Democratic Republic, Hungary, Iraq, Libya, Poland, USSR and South Yemen. *Hind-E:* USSR

First flight 1975

Single-seat close-support fighter

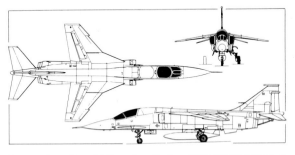

Power plant: Two Ishikawajima-Harima TF40-IHI-801A (licence-

built Rolls-Royce Turboméca Adour Mk 801A) turbofan engines (each 7 070 lb; 3 207 kg st with afterburning)
Wing span: 25 ft 10¼ in (7.88 m)
Length overall: 58 ft 6¼ in (17.84 m)
Max T-O weight: 30 146 lb (13 674 kg)
Max level speed: Mach 1.6 (917 knots; 1 056 mph; 1 700 km/h) at 36 000 ft (11 000 m)
Time to 36 000 ft (11 000 m): 2 min
Typical combat radius: hi-lo-hi with two Mitsubishi ASM-1 anti-ship missiles and external fuel tank, 300 nm (346 miles; 556 km); with four air-to-air missiles, 150 nm (172 miles; 278 km)
Armament: One 20 mm Vulcan JM61 multi-barrel gun. Four stores pylons under wings and one under fuselage for up to 6 000 lb (2 720 kg) of 250, 500 or 750 lb bombs, or rockets, air-to-air missiles or anti-ship missiles. Two further Sidewinder air-to-air missiles can be carried on wingtip launchers
In service with: Japan Air Self-Defence Force

First flight 1953

NATO Reporting Name *Bison*
Long-range reconnaissance-bomber

Photo and Drawing: *Bison-C*
Data: *Bison-A,* estimated

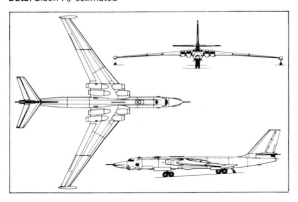

Power plant: Four Mikulin AM-3D turbojet engines (each 19 180 lb; 8 700 kg st)

Wing span: 165 ft 7½ in (50.48 m)
Length overall: 154 ft 10 in (47.20 m)
Max T-O weight: 350 000 lb (158 750 kg)
Max level speed at 36 000 ft (11 000 m): 486 knots (560 mph; 901 km/h)
Service ceiling: 45 000 ft (13 700 m)
Unrefuelled range with 10 000 lb (4 535 kg) bombs: at 452 knots (520 mph; 837 km/h): 6 080 nm (7 000 miles; 11 265 km)
Armament: Ten 23 mm guns in twin-gun turrets above fuselage fore and aft of wing, under fuselage fore and aft of weapon bays, and in tail. Three weapon bays in centre-fuselage
Variants:
Bison-A: Long-range strategic bomber, described above, with internal bomb bays for free-fall nuclear or conventional weapons. In 1980, only 43 remained in service as strategic bombers; 31 more were equipped as flight refuelling tankers
Bison-B: Maritime reconnaissance version. Glazed nose of *Bison-A* replaced by 'solid' nose with large superimposed flight refuelling probe. Underfuselage blister fairings over avionic equipment. Armament reduced by removal of aft gun turrets above and below fuselage. Few remain
Bison-C: Similar to *Bison-B* except for large search radar faired into longer nose, aft of centrally-mounted flight refuelling probe. Few remain
In service with: Soviet Air Force and Navy

First flight early 1970s

NANCHANG A-5 (China)

NATO Reporting Name *Fantan-A*
Single-seat fighter-bomber, derived from F-6/MiG-19

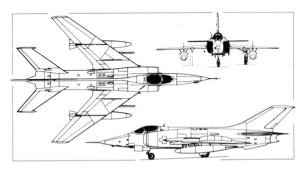

Power plant: Two Shenyang-built Tumansky RD-9B-811 turbojet engines (each 8 267 lb; 3 750 kg st with afterburning)
Wing span: 33 ft 5 in (10.20 m)
Length overall: 50 ft 0 in (15.25 m)
Max T-O weight: 23 590 lb (10 700 kg)
Max level speed at height: 1 145 knots (1 320 mph; 2 125 km/h)
Service ceiling: 52 500 ft (16 000 m)
Combat radius: up to 430 nm (500 miles; 800 km)
Armament: Two 30 mm cannon in wing roots. Four underwing hardpoints for two 500 kg or four 250 kg bombs, two 250 kg bombs and two drop-tanks, two short-range infra-red homing missiles of the *Atoll* type, or four eight-round packs of 57 mm air-to-surface rockets. Fuselage weapons bay for about 3 300 lb (1 500 kg) of stores, with external stores racks to each side
In service with: Chinese Air Force and Navy (A-5 is Western designation; Chinese designation is *Q-5*)

First flight 1947

Single-seat tactical fighter and fighter-bomber

Photo, Drawing and Data: F-86F Sabre

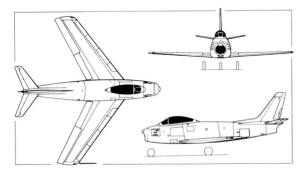

Power plant: One General Electric J47-GE-27 turbojet engine (5 970 lb; 2 708 kg st)
Wing span: 39 ft 1 in (11.91 m)
Length overall: 37 ft 6½ in (11.44 m)
Max T-O weight: 20 610 lb (9 350 kg)
Max level speed at S/L: 597 knots (687 mph; 1 105 km/h)

Range at 460 knots (530 mph; 853 km/h): 803 nm (925 miles; 1 485 km)
Armament: Six 0.50 in Colt-Browning machine-guns in nose. Provision for two Sidewinder missiles, two 1 000 lb bombs or eight rockets under wings
Variants in current use:
F-86D: Single-seat all-weather interceptor; lengthened nose with radome above intake; twenty-four 2.75 in rockets in retractable ventral pack; no guns; wing span 37 ft 1½ in (11.32 m); J47-GE-17, GE-17B or GE-33 afterburning engine
F-86F: Day fighter and fighter-bomber (see data)
F-86K: Fiat licence version of F-86D, with four 20 mm cannon and two Sidewinders instead of fuselage rockets; GE-17B engine (7 500 lb; 3 402 kg st with afterburning); span increased later to 39 ft 1 in (11.91 m)
F-86L: Converted from F-86D; extended span (39 ft 1 in; 11.91 m), updated avionics
Canadair Sabre Mk 6: Canadian licence-built version with Orenda 14 engine (7 275 lb; 3 300 kg st)
Commonwealth Sabre Mk 32: Australian licence version; Rolls-Royce Avon 26 engine (7 500 lb; 3 402 kg st); two 30 mm Aden cannon, and two Sidewinders or 500 lb bombs or drop-tanks
In service with: Air forces of Bolivia (F-86F), Honduras (F-86F), Indonesia (Commonwealth Sabre Mk 32), South Korea (F-86D and F-86F), Pakistan (Canadair Sabre Mk 6), Venezuela (F-86K) and Yugoslavia (F-86D and F-86L)

First flight 1953

Single-seat interceptor and fighter-bomber

Photo, Drawing and Data: F-100D Super Sabre

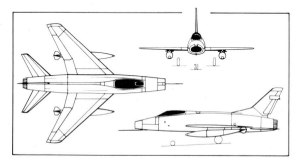

Power plant: One Pratt & Whitney J57-P-21A turbojet engine (17 000 lb; 7 710 kg st with afterburning)
Wing span: 38 ft 9 in (11.81 m)

NORTH AMERICAN F-100 SUPER SABRE (USA)

Length overall: 54 ft 3 in (16.54 m) incl probe
Max T-O weight: 34 832 lb (15 800 kg)
Max level speed at 36 000 ft (11 000 m): 750 knots (864 mph; 1 390 km/h)
Range with two external tanks: 1 300 nm (1 500 miles; 2 410 km)
Armament: Four 20 mm cannon in fuselage. Six underwing pylons for air-to-air or air-to-surface missiles, bombs, rockets etc
Variants in current service:
F-100A: Initial production version. Single-seat day fighter; J57-P-7 or P-39 engine (9 700 lb; 4 400 kg st), four 20 mm M39E cannon, six hardpoints for external stores
F-100C: Single-seat fighter-bomber; strengthened wings, with up to 7 500 lb (3 402 kg) of external weapons on eight hardpoints; in-flight refuelling capability. Power plant as F-100D
F-100D: Design refinements, including taller fin. Four 20 mm cannon, four Sidewinders, 7 500 lb (3 402 kg) of external weapons or two Bullpup missiles
F-100F: Tandem two-seat operational trainer/tactical attack version. Two 20 mm cannon, 6 000 lb (2 722 kg) of external weapons. Fuselage lengthened by 3 ft 0 in (0.91 m)
In service with: Air forces of Denmark (F-100D and F-100F), Taiwan (F-100A and F-100F) and Turkey (F-100C and F-100F)

Lightweight tactical fighter, fighter/trainer and reconnaissance aircraft
Photo, Drawing and Data F-5A

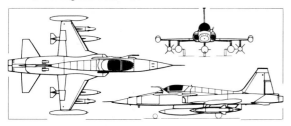

Power plant: Two General Electric J85-GE-13 turbojet engines (each 4 080 lb; 1 850 kg st with afterburning)
Wing span: 25 ft 3 in (7.70 m)
Length overall: 47 ft 2 in (14.38 m)
Max T-O weight: 20 677 lb (9 379 kg)
Max level speed at 36 000 ft (11 000 m): at AUW of 11 450 lb (5 193 kg): 803 knots (925 mph; 1 488 km/h)
Rate of climb at S/L, AUW as above: 28 700 ft (8 750 m)/min
Service ceiling, AUW as above: 50 500 ft (15 390 m)
Range with max fuel, AUW as above: with reserve fuel for 20 min max endurance at S/L, tanks retained: 1 205 nm (1 387 miles; 2 232 km)
Combat radius with max payload, AUW as above: allowances for 20 min max endurance at S/L and 5 min combat at S/L: 170 nm (195 miles; 314 km)

Armament: Two Sidewinder missiles on wingtip launchers and two 20 mm Colt-Browning M39 guns in fuselage nose. A bomb of more than 2 000 lb (910 kg) or high-rate-of-fire gun pack can be suspended from underfuselage pylon. Four underwing points for four air-to-air missiles, Bullpup air-to-surface missiles, bombs, up to 20 air-to-surface rockets, gun packs or external fuel tanks. Reconnaissance nose does not eliminate 20 mm nose gun capability
Variants:
F-5A: Single-seat version (see data). Those for Canada, Netherlands, Norway and Spain designated *CF-5A, NF-5A, F-5G* (not to be confused with new single-engined F-5G on page 197) and *SF-5A* respectively; CF and NF models have modified landing gear and other improvements
RF-5A: Photo-reconnaissance version of F-5A, with four cameras in modified nose. Norwegian version designated *RF-5G*
F-5B: Tandem two-seat operational or trainer version. Similar external weapons capability to F-5A, but two 20 mm nose guns deleted. Those for Canada, Netherlands, Norway and Spain designated *CF-5D, NF-5D, F-5T and SF-5B*
In service with: Air forces of Canada (CF-5A and CF-5D), Ethiopia (F-5A and F-5B), Greece (F-5A, RF-5A and F-5B), Jordan (F-5A and F-5B), South Korea (F-5A, RF-5A and F-5B), Morocco (F-5A, RF-5A and F-5B), Netherlands (NF-5A and NF-5D), Norway (F-5G, RF-5G and F-5T), Philippines (F-5A and F-5B), Spain (RF-5A, SF-5A and SF-5B), Taiwan (F-5A and F-5B), Thailand (F-5A, RF-5A and F-5B), Turkey (F-5A, RF-5A and F-5B), Venezuela (CF-5A and CF-5D), Viet-Nam (F-5A) and Yemen Arab Republic (F-5B)

See also Tiger II overleaf

Lightweight tactical fighter, fighter/trainer and reconnaissance aircraft

Photo, Drawing and Data: F-5E

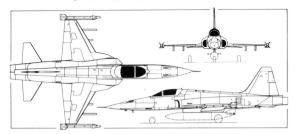

Power plant: Two General Electric J85-GE-21A turbojet engines (each 5 000 lb; 2 267 kg st with afterburning)
Wing span: 26 ft 8 in (8.13 m)
Length overall: 48 ft 2 in (14.68 m)
Max T-O weight: 24 676 lb (11 193 kg)
Max level speed at 36 000 ft (11 000 m): at AUW of 13 350 lb (6 055 kg): Mach 1.63 (934 knots; 1 076 mph; 1 732 km/h)
Max rate of climb at S/L, at above AUW: 34 500 ft (10 516 m)/min
Service ceiling, at above AUW: 51 800 ft (15 790 m)
Range with max fuel, at above AUW: with reserve fuel for 20 min at S/L, tanks retained: 1 340 nm (1 543 miles; 2 483 km)
Combat radius, at above AUW, with two Sidewinder missiles and max fuel: allowances as above and 5 min combat with max afterburning at 15 000 ft (4 570 m): 570 nm (656 miles; 1 056 km)

Armament: Two AIM-9 Sidewinder missiles on wingtip launchers. Two M39A2 20 mm cannon in nose. Up to 7 000 lb (3 175 kg) of mixed ordnance on four underwing and one underfuselage stations, including M129 leaflet bombs; Mk 82 GP and Snakeye 500 lb bombs; Mk 36 destructors; Mk 84 2 000 lb bombs; BLU-1, -27 or -32 U or F napalm; LAU-68 (7) 2.75 in rockets; LAU-3 (19) 2.75 in rockets; CBU-24, -49, -52 or -58 cluster bomb units; SUU-20 bomb and rocket packs; SUU-25 flare dispensers. Optional weapons include Maverick guided missiles, laser-guided bombs and a 30 mm underbelly gun pod

Variants:
F-5E: Advanced development of F-5A (which see). Standard single-seat version, also licence-built by AIDC in Taiwan. Large dorsal fin on Brazilian aircraft
RF-5E: Photo-reconnaissance version of F-5E, with various cameras, infra-red and laser linescanners in modified nose and advanced navigation equipment. Armament retained
F-5F: Tandem two-seat fighter/trainer version of F-5E. Fuselage lengthened by 3 ft 6½ in (1.08 m). One 20 mm gun deleted
F-5G: High-performance development of F-5E, powered by one General Electric F404-GE-400 afterburning turbofan (16 000 lb; 7 257 kg st). First flight in 1981. (Same designation applied to Norwegian Air Force F-5A; see previous entry)

In service with: Air forces of Brazil (F-5E), Chile (F-5E and F-5F), Ethiopia (F-5E), Indonesia (F-5E and F-5F), Iran (F-5E and F-5F), Jordan (F-5E and F-5F), Kenya (F-5E and F-5F), South Korea (F-5E and F-5F), Malaysia (F-5E and F-5F), Morocco (F-5E), Saudi Arabia (F-5E and F-5F), Singapore (F-5E and F-5F), Switzerland (F-5E and F-5F), Taiwan (F-5E and F-5F), Thailand (F-5E and F-5F), US Air Force and Navy (F-5E for 'Aggressor' training) and Viet-Nam (F-5E)

Tandem two-seat multi-role combat aircraft. Designed to fulfil six principal roles; close air support/battlefield interdiction; interdiction/counter air strike; air superiority; interception; naval strike; and reconnaissance

Photo and Data: Tornado IDS (Italian)
Drawing: Tornado ADV (F Mk 2)

Power plant: Two Turbo-Union RB.199-34R-04 turbofan engines (each 16 000 lb; 7 257 kg st with afterburning)
Wing span: spread 45 ft 7¼ in (13.90 m); swept 28 ft 2½ in (8.60 m)
Length overall: 54 ft 9½ in (16.70 m)
Height overall: 18 ft 8½ in (5.70 m)
Max T-O weight: 58 400 lb (26 490 kg)
Max level speed at 36 000 ft (11 000 m): 'clean' Mach 2.2 (1 261 knots; 1 452 mph; 2 337 km/h)
Max level speed at low altitude: above 800 knots (920 mph; 1 480 km/h) IAS; with external stores Mach 0.92 (600 knots; 691 mph; 1 112 km/h)
Time to 30 000 ft (9 145 m): less than 2 min
Radius of action with heavy weapons load: hi-lo-lo-hi 750 nm (863 miles; 1 390 km)
Armament: Two 27 mm Mauser cannon in lower front fuselage. Three hardpoints under fuselage, and up to four swivelling attachments under outer wings, for externally-mounted stores. These vary according to version, with emphasis on ability to carry a wide range of non-nuclear weapons. Among those already specified for, or suitable for carriage by, the IDS Tornado are the Sparrow and Sidewinder air-to-air missiles; AS.30, Martel, Kormoran and Sea Eagle air-to-surface missiles; napalm; BL-755 600 lb cluster bombs; MW-1 munitions dispenser; 1 000 lb bombs and smart or retarded bombs, plus active or passive ECM pods

Variants:

Tornado IDS (RAF GR Mk 1): Interdictor/strike version, as described. First flown on 14 August 1974; to become operational in 1982. Max weapons load 18 000 lb (8 165 kg)

Tornado ADV (RAF F Mk 2): Air defence variant. Fuselage lengthened by 4 ft 5½ in (1.36 m). Sweep increased on fixed portion of wings, to extend chord. Marconi Foxhunter track-while-scan pulse-Doppler radar. Avionics include ESM, ECCM, radar warning receiver, low light-level TV for target identification. Armament comprises one 27 mm Mauser cannon, four Sky Flash and two Sidewinder missiles. First flown on 27 October 1979; to become operational in 1984

In production for: Air forces of German Federal Republic (212 IDS for Air Force, 112 for Navy), Italy (100 IDS), and UK (220 IDS, 165 ADV)

Tandem two-seat observation and counter-insurgency aircraft (OV-10A/C/D/E/F) and target tug (OV-10B and OV-10B(Z))

Photo: OV-10D Bronco
Drawing and Data: OV-10A Bronco

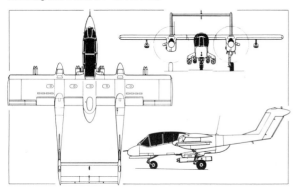

Power plant: Two Garrett T76-G-416/417 turboprop engines (each 715 ehp)
Wing span: 40 ft 0 in (12.19 m)
Length overall: 41 ft 7 in (12.67 m)
Overload T-O weight: 14 444 lb (6 552 kg)
Max level speed at S/L, without weapons: 244 knots (281 mph; 452 km/h)

Max rate of climb at S/L: at AUW of 9 908 lb (4 494 kg): 2 600 ft (790 m)/min
Combat radius with max weapon load, no loiter: 198 nm (228 miles; 367 km)
Ferry range with auxiliary fuel: 1 200 nm (1 382 miles; 2 224 km)
Armament: Four 600 lb (272 kg) weapon attachment points under short sponsons extending from each side of lower-fuselage. Fifth attachment point, capacity 1 200 lb (544 kg), under centre-fuselage. Two 7.62 mm M60C machine-guns carried in each sponson. Provision for one Sidewinder missile on each wing

Variants:

OV-10A: Initial production version for USAF/USN/USMC (see data). Six transferred to Royal Moroccan Air Force
OV-10B: Similar to OV-10A, for Germany for target towing
OV-10B(Z): As OV-10B, but with J85-GE-4 auxiliary turbojet (2 950 lb; 1 338 kg st) above central nacelle; for Germany
OV-10C: Version of OV-10A for Thailand
OV-10D: NOS (Night Observation/Surveillance) version, converted from OV-10A. Optional 20 mm gun turret under rear fuselage. Forward-looking infra-red sensor under lengthened nose, laser target designator within FLIR turret. Various rocket pods, flare pods and free-fall stores on pylons at Sidewinder missile stations. Uprated (1 040 shp) engines; provision for drop-tanks on stores pylons. For USMC
OV-10E: Similar to OV-10A, for Venezuela
OV-10F: Similar to OV-10A, for Indonesia
In service with: Air forces of German Federal Republic, Indonesia, Morocco, Philippines, Thailand, USA (Air Force and Marine Corps) and Venezuela

Single-seat fighter and reconnaissance aircraft and tandem two-seat operational trainer
Drawing: J 35F Draken
Photo and Data: Saab 35S Draken

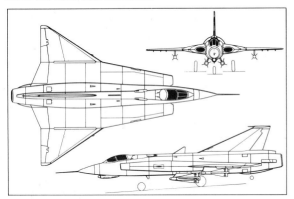

Power plant: One Volvo Flygmotor RM6C (Rolls-Royce Avon 300-series) turbojet engine (17 650 lb; 8 000 kg st with afterburning)
Wing span: 30 ft 10 in (9.40 m)
Length overall: 50 ft 4 in (15.35 m)
Max overload T-O weight: 35 275 lb (16 000 kg)
Max level speed with afterburning at 25 130 lb (11 400 kg) AUW: 1 146 knots (1 320 mph; 2 124 km/h)

Max rate of climb at S/L with afterburning: at above AUW: 34 450 ft (10 500 m)/min
Radius of action (hi-lo-hi), internal fuel only: at above AUW: 343 nm (395 miles; 635 km)
Radius of action (hi-lo-hi) with two 1 000 lb bombs, two drop-tanks and AUW of 32 165 lb (14 590 kg): 541 nm (623 miles; 1 003 km)
Armament: Nine attachment points (each 1 000 lb; 454 kg) for external stores; three under each wing and three under fuselage. Stores can consist of air-to-air missiles and pods of unguided air-to-air rockets (19 × 7.5 cm), 12 × 13.5 cm Bofors air-to-ground rockets, nine 1 000 lb bombs or fourteen 500 lb bombs, or fuel tanks. Two or four RB24 (Sidewinder) air-to-air missiles can be carried under wings and fuselage. Two 30 mm Aden cannon (one in each wing) can be replaced by extra internal fuel tanks. With two 280 Imp gallon (1 275 litre) and two 110 Imp gallon (500 litre) drop-tanks, two 1 000 lb or four 500 lb bombs can be carried

Variants in current service:
J 35F: Single-seat all-weather fighter. Final Swedish Air Force production version: improved fire control system for single 30 mm Aden cannon and two or four Hughes Falcon air-to-air missiles
SK 35C: Tandem two-seat operational trainer
Saab 35X: Export version (35XD for Denmark, 35S for Finland) for tactical strike and reconnaissance. Increased internal fuel and external weapons load (maximum 9 920 lb; 4 500 kg). Danish Air Force designations *F-35* (fighter), *RF-35* (reconnaissance, with cameras in nose) and TF-35 (trainer)
In service with: Air forces of Denmark (F-35, RF-35 and TF-35), Finland (Saab 35S, J 35BS, J 35F and SK 35C) and Sweden (J 35F/SK 35C)

Single-seat attack/interceptor, interceptor/attack, photo-reconnaissance and sea surveillance aircraft, and tandem two-seat operational trainer

Photo: JA 37 Viggen
Drawing: JA 37 Viggen, with additional side view of SK 37
Data: AJ 37 Viggen

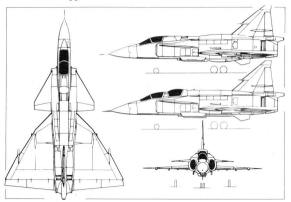

Power plant: One Volvo Flygmotor RM 8A (supersonic development of the Pratt & Whitney JT8D-22) turbofan engine (26 015 lb; 11 800 kg st with afterburning)
Wing span: 34 ft 9¼ in (10.60 m)
Length overall (incl probe): 53 ft 5¾ in (16.30 m)

Max T-O weight: 45 195 lb (20 500 kg)
Max level speed: at high altitude: 1 146 knots (1 320 mph; 2 124 km/h); at 330 ft (100 m): above 726 knots (836 mph; 1 346 km/h)
Time to 32 800 ft (10 000 m): less than 1 min 40 s
Tactical radius with external armament: hi-lo-hi: over 540 nm (620 miles; 1 000 km); lo-lo-lo: over 270 nm (310 miles; 500 km)
Armament: All armament is carried normally on seven hardpoints, three under fuselage and two under each wing. Primary armament of air-to-surface missiles, including the Swedish RB04E and RB05A and the TV-guided Maverick, plus various types of air-to-surface rockets, bombs and 30 mm Aden gun pods. AJ37 can be adapted to perform interception missions armed with RB24 (Sidewinder) or RB28 (Falcon) air-to-air missiles

Variants:
AJ 37: All-weather attack (secondary interceptor) version (see data)
JA 37: All-weather interceptor (secondary attack) version. Uprated RM8B engine (28 108 lb; 12 750 kg st with afterburning), 30 mm Oerlikon long-range cannon in ventral pack, improved fire control and other avionics, RB71 Sky Flash and Sidewinder air-to-air missiles, and taller fin. Optional attack armament comprises four packs of 135 mm rockets
SF 37: Photo-reconnaissance version. Modified nose with seven cameras, infra-red sensor, ECM etc. Provision for two underwing Sidewinder air-to-air missiles for self-defence
SH 37: Maritime reconnaissance version. Nose radar similar to AJ 37, with recording camera; active or passive ECM pods; ECM registration equipment; Sidewinder air-to-air missiles underwing
SK 37: Tandem two-seat operational trainer. Rear cockpit 'stepped'. Taller fin. Capable of attack role, with AJ 37 armament
In service with: Swedish Air Force (all versions)

First flight 1963

Side-by-side two-seat basic trainer and light attack aircraft

Photo: SK 60C
Drawing and Data: Saab 105XT

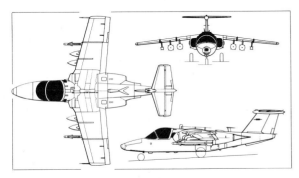

Power plant: Two General Electric J85-GE-17B turbojet engines (each 2 850 lb; 1 293 kg st)
Wing span: 31 ft 2 in (9.50 m)
Length overall: 35 ft 5¼ in (10.80 m)
Max T-O weight, with armament: 14 330 lb (6 500 kg)
Max level speed at S/L: at max T-O weight: 524 knots (603 mph; 970 km/h)
Range at 43 000 ft (13 100 m) at 378 knots (435 mph; 700 km/h):

with external tanks and 30 min reserves: 1 580 nm (1 820 miles; 2 930 km)
Typical attack radius, including reserves, with 3 000 lb (1 360 kg) bomb load: hi-lo-hi: 420 nm (484 miles; 780 km); lo-lo-lo: 167 nm (192 miles; 310 km)
Armament: Three attachment points under each wing, the inner and outer points each capable of supporting a 610 lb (275 kg) load and the centre points each capable of supporting 1 000 lb (454 kg). Total weapons load 4 410 lb (2 000 kg), increased to 5 180 lb (2 350 kg) on Saab 105G. Wide range of weapons includes two 1 000 lb and four 500 lb bombs; four 500 lb bombs and two 30 mm gun pods; four 500 lb napalm bombs and two Minigun pods; twelve 13.5 cm rockets; six pods each containing four 5 in rockets; eighteen 7.5 cm rockets; two Saab RB05 air-to-surface and two infra-red (Sidewinder) air-to-air missiles and two Minigun pods
Variants:
SK 60A/B: Basic trainers with limited (SK 60A) or full (SK 60B) capability for adaptation to light attack with underwing-mounted weapons. Turboméca Aubisque turbofan engines (each 1 640 lb; 743 kg st)
SK 60C: Variant of SK 60B with panoramic camera in modified nose; attack capability retained
Saab 105O: Export version for Austria, based on 105XT prototype (see data). More powerful engines, higher performance, increased weapon load
Saab 105G: Further development of 105O; max weapon load (with reduced fuel) increased to 5 180 lb (2 350 kg); upgraded avionics and equipment. Prototype only
In service with: Air forces of Austria (105Ö) and Sweden (SK 60A/B/C)

Single-seat tactical support aircraft and tandem two-seat advanced or operational trainer

Photo, Drawing and Data: Jaguar GR Mk 1

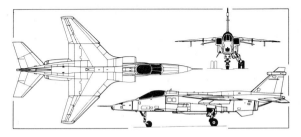

Power plant: Two Rolls-Royce Turboméca Adour Mk 102 turbofan engines (each 7 305 lb; 3 313 kg st with afterburning) in French aircraft; Adour Mk 104 (8 040 lb; 3 647 kg st) in most RAF aircraft
Wing span: 28 ft 6 in (8.69 m)
Length overall: 55 ft 2½ in (16.83 m)
Max T-O weight: 34 612 lb (15 700 kg)
Max level speed: at S/L: Mach 1.1 (729 knots; 840 mph; 1 350 km/h); at 36 000 ft (11 000 m): Mach 1.6 (917 knots; 1 056 mph; 1 699 km/h)
Typical attack radius: internal fuel only: 310-440 nm (357-507 miles; 575-815 km); with external fuel: 490-760 nm (564-875 miles; 908-1 408 km)
Armament: Two 30 mm cannon in fuselage; 10 000 lb (4 535 kg) max external load of bombs, rockets, air-to-air missiles, photo-flares, reconnaissance pack or drop-tanks on one underfuselage attachment and four under wings
Variants:
Jaguar A: French single-seat tactical version; DEFA cannon and primarily French equipment (basically that of E, plus panoramic camera, Doppler radar, navigation computer etc). Some carry AN 52 tactical nuclear weapon
Jaguar B (RAF T Mk 2): British two-seat operational trainer. Generally similar to Jaguar E except for primarily British equipment
Jaguar E: French two-seat advanced trainer
Jaguar S (RAF GR Mk 1): British single-seat tactical version. Generally similar to Jaguar A but with computer-controlled inertial navigation and weapon-aiming system, and laser rangefinder and marked target seeker in modified nose. Aden cannon and primarily British equipment
Jaguar International: Export version. Similar to Jaguar S but with Adour Mk 804 turbofans (each 8 040 lb; 3 647 kg st with afterburning) or Adour Mk 811 (8 400 lb; 3 810 kg st). Options include over-wing missile pylons, multi-purpose nose radar, anti-shipping weapons and night sensors. Available also in maritime version. Max external weapons load 10 500 lb (4 763 kg)
In service with: Air forces of Ecuador (International), France (Jaguar A and E), India (International; RAF Jaguars on loan until deliveries begin), Oman (International) and UK (GR Mk 1 and T Mk 2)

STOL anti-submarine flying-boat (PS-1) and search and rescue amphibian (US-1)

Photo and Data: PS-1
Drawing: US-1

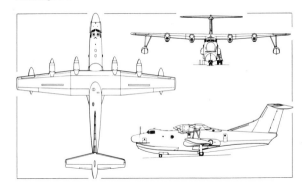

Power plant: Four Ishikawajima-built General Electric T64-IHI-10 turboprop engines (each 3 060 ehp)
Wing span: 108 ft 9 in (33.15 m)

Length overall: 109 ft 9¼ in (33.46 m)
Max T-O weight: 94 800 lb (43 000 kg)
Max level speed at 5 000 ft (1 525 m): at normal T-O weight of 79 365 lb (36 000 kg): 295 knots (340 mph; 547 km/h)
Max rate of climb at S/L: 2 264 ft (690 m)/min
Service ceiling: 29 500 ft (9 000 m)
Normal range: 1 169 nm (1 347 miles; 2 168 km)
Max endurance: 15 h
Accommodation: Flight crew of five (two pilots, navigator, engineer and radio operator), plus radar operator, MAD operator, two sonar operators and a tactical co-ordinator
Armament and equipment: No built-in armament. Two underwing pods, between engines, containing a total of four homing torpedoes; launcher under each wingtip for three 5 in air-to-surface rockets; dipping sonar; acoustic search and echo ranging gear in hull, with 20 sonobuoys, 12 explosive charges, four 330 lb bombs and smoke bombs; search radar in nose, MAD in retractable tail-boom, searchlight under starboard wing
Variants:
PS-1 (company designation SS-2): Anti-submarine flying-boat version (see data)
US-1 (company designation SS-2A): Search and rescue amphibian version; externally similar except for retractable tricycle landing gear. Operational equipment includes markers and launcher, two life-rafts, three lifebuoys, lifeboat with outboard motor, lifelines, 12 stretchers, flares etc
In service with: Japan (Navy, PS-1 and US-1)

First flight 1959

Anti-submarine, search and rescue and transport helicopter
Photo: Agusta-built SH-3D Sea King
Data: SH-3D Sea King
Drawing: SH-3H Sea King

Power plant: Two General Electric T58-GE-10 turboshaft engines (each 1 400 shp)
Main rotor diameter: 62 ft 0 in (18.90 m)
Length overall: 72 ft 8 in (22.15 m)
Normal T-O weight: 18 626 lb (8 450 kg)
Max level speed at 20 500 lb (9 300 kg) AUW: 144 knots (166 mph; 267 km/h)
Max rate of climb at S/L, at above AUW: 2 200 ft (670 m)/min
Service ceiling, at above AUW: 14 700 ft (4 480 m)
Range with max fuel, 10% reserves, at above AUW: 542 nm (625 miles; 1 005 km)
Accommodation: Pilot, co-pilot and two sonar operators

SIKORSKY S-61A/B and H-3 SEA KING (USA)

Armament: Provision for 840 lb (381 kg) of weapons, including homing torpedoes
Variants:
HH-3A: USN armed search and rescue; converted from SH-3A
RH-3A: USN minesweeper; converted from SH-3A
SH-3A: Initial USN anti-submarine version (originally HSS-2); 1 250 shp T58-GE-8B turboshafts
CH-124: Export SH-3A for Canada (originally CHSS-2)
S-61A: Export version for Denmark; long-range air/sea rescue, 26-troop transport or ambulance, based on SH-3A
S-61A-4 Nuri: Export version for Malaysia; 31-seat transport based on SH-3A. Similar version licence-built by Agusta in Italy, as AS-61A-4
SH-3D: USN improved ASW version; uprated engines etc (see data). Licence-built also by Agusta in Italy
VH-3D: USMC/Army VIP transport
S-61D-4: Export SH-3D for Argentina
SH-3G: USN utility version; converted from SH-3A (ASW equipment deleted)
SH-3H: USN anti-submarine/missile defence version; converted from SH-3A (new ASW equipment, plus ESM and new radar)
In service with: Air forces of Argentina (Navy, S-61D-4), Brazil (Navy, SH-3D), Canada (CH-124), Denmark (S-61A), Iran (Navy, Agusta-Sikorsky SH-3D), Italy (Air Force AS-61A-4; Navy, Agusta-Sikorsky SH-3D), Japan (Navy, HSS-2/2A), Malaysia (S-61A-4 Nuri), Peru (Navy, Agusta-Sikorsky SH-3D), Spain (Navy, Agusta-Sikorsky SH-3D), and USA (Navy, SH-3A/D, HH-3A, SH-3G and SH-3H; Marine Corps, VH-3D; Army, VH-3D)

See also Westland Sea King

First flight 1979

SIKORSKY S-70L/SH-60B SEAHAWK (USA)

Anti-submarine and anti-ship missile defence helicopter

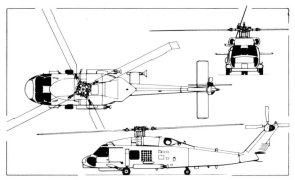

Power plant: Two General Electric T700-GE-401 turboshaft engines (each 1 690 shp)
Main rotor diameter: 53 ft 8 in (16.36 m)
Length overall: 64 ft 10 in (19.76 m) with rotors turning
Max T-O weight: 21 884 lb (9 926 kg)
Max cruising speed at 5 000 ft (1 525 m): 135 knots (155 mph; 249 km/h)
Max vertical rate of climb at S/L: 1 045 ft (319 m)/min
Accommodation: Pilot and co-pilot/airborne tactical officer on flight deck. Station for sensor operator in main cabin
Armament and equipment: Two Mk 46 torpedoes, Texas Instruments AN/ASQ-81 magnetic anomaly detector (MAD) and AN/APS-124 search radar, chin-mounted pods for ESM equipment, 25-tube pneumatic launcher for sonobuoys on port side, Hazeltine AN/APX-76A active IFF, rescue hoist, etc
Under development for: US Navy

First flight 1967

Single-seat light attack aircraft

Photo, Drawing and Data: J-1 Jastreb

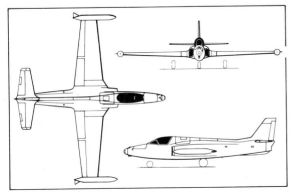

Power plant: One Rolls-Royce Viper Mk 531 turbojet engine (3 000 lb; 1 360 kg st)
Wing span over tip-tanks: 38 ft 4 in (11.68 m)
Length overall: 35 ft 8½ in (10.88 m)

Max T-O weight: 11 243 lb (5 100 kg)
Max level speed at 19 680 ft (6 000 m): at AUW of 8 748 lb (3 968 kg): 442 knots (510 mph; 820 km/h)
Max rate of climb at S/L, at above AUW: 4 135 ft (1 260 m)/min
Service ceiling, at above AUW: 39 375 ft (12 000 m)
Max range at 29 520 ft (9 000 m): with tip-tanks full: 820 nm (945 miles; 1 520 km)
Armament: Three 0.50 in Colt-Browning machine-guns in nose, with 135 rds/gun. Eight underwing weapon attachments. Two inboard attachments can carry two bombs of up to 250 kg each, two clusters of small bombs, two 200 litre napalm tanks, two pods each with 12 or 16 × 57 mm or four 127 mm rockets, or two 45 kg photo flares. Other attachments can each carry a 127 mm rocket
Variants:
J-1: Standard Yugoslav Air Force version, as described
J-1-E: Export version, with updated equipment
RJ-1: Tactical reconnaissance version for Yugoslav Air Force. Cameras in fuselage and nose of each tip-tank
RJ-1-E: Export reconnaissance version. Daylight system comprises three Vinten 360/140A cameras, in nose of each tip-tank and in fuselage. Night system has Vinten 1025/527 camera in fuselage. Flash bombs or H E bombs on underwing hardpoints
TJ-1: Tandem two-seat operational conversion trainer; full operational capability
In service with: Air forces of Yugoslavia (J-1, RJ-1 and TJ-1) and Zambia (J-1-E, RJ-1-E and TJ-1)

First flight 1974

SOKO/CNIAR ORAO/IAR-93 (EAGLE) (International)

Single-seat tactical fighter and two-seat operational trainer

Photo, Drawing and Data: Single-seat fighter version

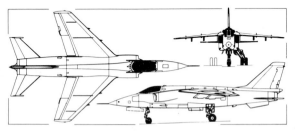

Power plant: Two Rolls-Royce Viper Mk 632-41 turbojet engines (each 5 008 lb; 2 271 kg st with afterburning)

Wing span: 31 ft 7⅛ in (9.63 m)
Length overall: 48 ft 9⅞ in (14.88 m)
Max T-O weight: 23 148 lb (10 500 kg)
Max level speed, 'clean': 610 knots (702 mph; 1 130 km/h) at low level
Max rate of climb at S/L at AUW of 18 959 lb (8 600 kg): 14 882 ft (4 536 m)/min
Service ceiling: 42 650 ft (13 000 m)
Armament: Two 23 mm cannon in lower front fuselage. Provision for approx 5 510 lb (2 500 kg) of external stores
Variants:
Developed in both single-seat and two-seat versions. Prototypes have non-afterburning engines. Specification figures quoted are estimated for production aircraft, which will have afterburners
In production for: Air forces of Romania (as IAR-93) and Yugoslavia (as Orao)

First flight about 1956

NATO Reporting Names *Fitter-A* and *Moujik*
Single-seat ground attack fighter
Photo and Data: Su-7B
Drawing: Su-7BM

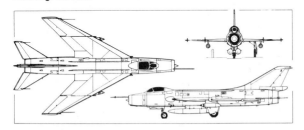

Power plant: One Lyulka AL-7F-1 turbojet engine (22 046 lb; 10 000 kg st with afterburning). Two JATO rockets can be fitted under rear fuselage to shorten take-off run
Wing span: 29 ft 3½ in (8.93 m)
Length overall, incl probe: 57 ft 0 in (17.37 m)
Max T-O weight: 29 750 lb (13 500 kg)

Max level speed at 36 000 ft (11 000 m): 'clean': Mach 1.6 (917 knots; 1 055 mph; 1 700 km/h); with external stores Mach 1.2 (685 knots; 788 mph; 1 270 km/h)
Max level speed at S/L without afterburning: 460 knots (530 mph; 850 km/h)
Rate of climb at S/L: approx 29 900 ft (9 120 m)/min
Service ceiling: 49 700 ft (15 150 m)
Combat radius: 172-260 nm (200-300 miles; 320-480 km)
Max range: 780 nm (900 miles; 1 450 km)
Armament: Attachments for external stores, including rocket packs, nuclear and H E bombs (usually two 750 kg and two 500 kg), under each wing. A pair of external fuel tanks can be carried under the centre-fuselage, but these reduce the max external weapon load to 2 200 lb (1 000 kg). A 30 mm NR-30 cannon is installed in each wing-root leading-edge
Variants:
Su-7B: Basic single-seater, as described
Su-7BM: Modified version. Low-pressure nosewheel tyre, requiring blistered doors
Su-7U (Moujik): Tandem two-seat training version
In service with: Air forces of Afghanistan, Algeria, Czechoslovakia, Egypt, Hungary, India, Iraq, North Korea, Poland, Romania, Syria, USSR, Viet-Nam and South Yemen

First flight about 1956

NATO Reporting Names *Fishpot* and *Maiden*
Single-seat all-weather fighter and two-seat operational trainer

Photo: Su-9 *Fishpot-B*
Drawing and Data: Su-11 *Fishpot-C*

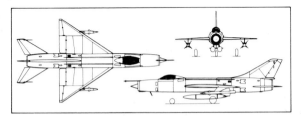

Power plant: One Lyulka AL-7F-1 turbojet engine (22 046 lb; 10 000 kg st with afterburning)
Wing span: 27 ft 8 in (8.43 m)

Length overall, incl probe: 56 ft 0 in (17.00 m)
Max T-O weight: approx 30 000 lb (13 600 kg)
Max level speed at 36 000 ft (11 000 m) (estimated): Mach 1.8 (1 033 knots; 1 190 mph; 1 915 km/h)
Service ceiling: 55 700 ft (16 975 m)
Armament: Two *Anab* missiles under wings, one with radar homing head and one with infra-red homing head
Variants:
Fishpot-A: Prototype, with small conical radome above chin air intake. Displayed in 1956
Su-9 (Fishpot-B): Initial production version, with radar in centre-body inside air intake. Lyulka AL-7F engine (19 840 lb; 9 000 kg st). R1L (NATO *Spin Scan*) radar. Armed with four *Alkali* air-to-air missiles. No guns
Su-11 (Fishpot-C): Improved version of Su-9, as described above. Uprated engine. Larger Uragan 5B (NATO *Skip Spin*) radar and air intake. Two duct fairings above fuselage, as on Su-7B. Much improved missile armament
Maiden: Tandem two-seat training version
In service with: Soviet Air Force

NATO Reporting Name *Flagon*
Single-seat supersonic interceptor and two-seat operational trainer

Photo: *Flagon-F*
Drawing: *Flagon-F,* with additional side views of *Flagon-C* (centre) and *Flagon-D* (top)
Data: *Flagon-F,* estimated

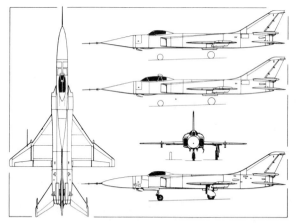

Power plant: Two afterburning turbojets, with variable-area nozzles, mounted side by side in rear fuselage. Reported to be Tumansky R-13F2-300s (each 15 875 lb; 7 200 kg st)
Wing span: 34 ft 6 in (10.53 m)
Length overall: 68 ft 0 in (20.50 m)
Max T-O weight: 35 275 lb (16 000 kg)
Max level speed above 36 000 ft (11 000 m): Mach 2.3 (1 320 knots; 1 520 mph; 2 445 km/h) with external stores; Mach 2.5 'clean'
Service ceiling: 65 600 ft (20 000 m)
Combat radius: 390 nm (450 miles; 725 km)
Armament: Single pylon for external store under each wing. Normal armament comprises one radar homing and one infra-red homing *Anab* air-to-air missile. Side-by-side pylons under centre-fuselage for further weapons or external fuel tanks
Variants:
Flagon-A: Basic single-seater, with simple delta wings identical in form to those of Su-11. Span 30 ft 0 in (9.15 m). Engines reported to be Tumansky R-11F2-300s (each 13 668 lb; 6 200 kg st)
Flagon-B: Experimental STOL version, for research only
Flagon-C: Two-seat training version of *Flagon-D,* with probable combat capability
Flagon-D: Similar to *Flagon-A* but with longer-span wings of compound sweep, produced by reducing the sweepback at the tips via a narrow unswept section. Conical radome retained. First major production version
Flagon-E: Wings as for *Flagon-D.* More powerful engines (reportedly R-13F-300s, each 14 550 lb; 6 600 kg st), increasing speed and range. Uprated avionics. Operational since second half of 1973
Flagon-F: Latest version, identified in service 1977. Similar to *Flagon-E* but with new ogival nose radome and uprated engines
In service with: Soviet Air Force

NATO Reporting Names *Fitter-C, D, E, F, G and H*
Single-seat and two-seat multi-role combat and training aircraft

Photo: *Fitter-E* (left) and *Fitter-H*
Photo and Data: Su-17 *Fitter-C*
Drawing: *Fitter-H*

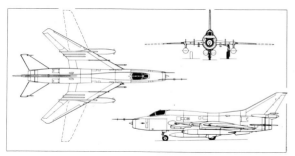

Power plant: One Lyulka AL-21F-3 turbojet engine (24 500 lb; 11 113 kg st with afterburning)
Wing span: spread: 45 ft 11¼ in (14.00 m); swept: 34 ft 9½ in (10.60 m)
Length overall, incl probes: 61 ft 6¼ in (18.75 m)
Max T-O weight: 39 020 lb (17 700 kg)

Max level speed at 36 000 ft (11 000 m): 'clean' Mach 2.17 (1 245 knots; 1 432 mph; 2 305 km/h)
Max level speed at S/L: 'clean' Mach 1.05 (693 knots; 798 mph; 1 284 km/h)
Rate of climb at S/L: 45 275 ft (13 800 m)/min
Service ceiling: 59 050 ft (18 000 m)
Combat radius: 195-340 nm (225-390 miles; 360-630 km) with 4 410 lb (2 000 kg) external load
Armament: Eight attachments for external stores under fuselage and fixed portions of wings. Max load 11 025 lb (5 000 kg). Up to four drop-tanks on outboard and centre attachments. Provision for carrying bombs, including nuclear weapons, cluster bombs, rocket pods, napalm and AS-7 *Kerry* air-to-surface missiles. Two 30 mm NR-30 guns in wing roots
Variants:
Fitter-B: Prototype only. Differed from standard Su-7B only in having pivoted outer wing panels and associated fences
Su-17 (Fitter-C): Single-seat attack fighter for Soviet Air Force
Su-17 (Fitter-D): As *Fitter-C*, but with forward fuselage lengthened by about 15 in (38 cm), added undernose radome, and laser marked target seeker in intake centrebody
Fitter-E: Tandem two-seat trainer for Soviet Air Force. Generally similar to *Fitter-C* but entire fuselage forward of wing drooped slightly to improve view from rear seat. Port wing-root gun deleted
Fitter-F: Export counterpart of *Fitter-D*. Increased-diameter rear fuselage. Longer dorsal fin.
Fitter-G: Developed two-seater, with combat capability. Taller fin with straight top. Shallow ventral fin Starboard gun only. Laser target seeker fitted

(cont on page 229)

Sukhoi Su-24

SUKHOI Su-24 (USSR)

NATO Reporting Name *Fencer*
Side-by-side two-seat fighter-bomber

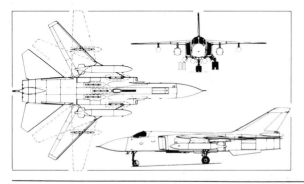

Power plant: Two afterburning turbojets: possibly Tumansky R-29B (each 25 350 lb; 11 500 kg st), or Lyulka AL-21F (each 25 000 lb; 11 340 kg st)
Wing span: spread: 56 ft 3 in (17.15 m); swept 31 ft 3 in (9.53 m)
Length overall: 69 ft 10 in (21.29 m)
Max T-O weight: 68 000 lb (30 850 kg)
Max level speed at height: above 1 150 knots (1 325 mph; 2 125 km/h)
Combat radius at S/L: over 175 nm (200 miles; 325 km)
Armament: One six-barrel 23 mm Gatling-type gun on port side of belly. Eight pylons under fuselage, wing-root gloves and outer wings for more than 15 000 lb (6 800 kg) of guided and unguided air-to-surface weapons, including nuclear weapons
In service with: Soviet Air Force

Sukhoi Su-17, -20, -22 *(cont from page 227)*

Fitter-H: Tactical reconnaissance fighter. As *Fitter-G* with drooped nose, but single-seat. Deep dorsal fairing aft of canopy
Aircraft supplied to other air forces have a lower equipment standard than those of the Soviet forces. In this case, the differences are such that new Sukhoi designations are allocated to them, as follows:
Su-20: Export counterpart of Soviet *Fitter-C*. Variations in rear fuselage contours by comparison with Su-17 suggest a different engine, possibly the Su-7's AL-7F-1

Su-22 (Fitter-C). Variant of Su-20. Further reduced equipment standard, with Sirena 2 limited-coverage radar warning receiver, virtually no navigation aids, and IFF incompatible with SA-3 (NATO *Goa*) surface-to-air missiles. Weapons include *Atoll* air-to-air missiles
In service with: Air forces of Algeria (Su-20), Czechoslovakia (Su-20), Egypt (Su-20), Iraq (Su-20), Peru (Su-22), Poland (Su-20), Syria (Su-22), USSR (Su-17), Viet-Nam, Yemen Arab Republic and South Yemen

Conversion of Cessna Model T337 'push and pull' twin-engined aircraft, for forward air control, helicopter escort, light ground attack, convoy protection, maritime patrol, personnel and freight transport, aerial photography, psychological warfare, medical evacuation and other duties

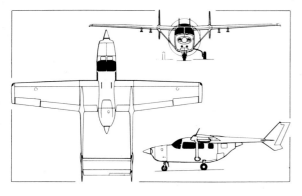

Power plant: Two 225 hp Continental TSIO-360 piston engines
Wing span: 38 ft 2 in (11.63 m)
Length overall: 29 ft 10 in (9.09 m)
Max T-O weight: 5 200 lb (2 359 kg)
Max level speed at 10 000 ft (3 050 m): 179 knots (206 mph; 332 km/h)
Max rate of climb at S/L: 1 100 ft (335 m)/min
Service ceiling: 28 500 ft (8 690 m)
Max range: 1 175 nm (1 353 miles; 2 177 km)
Accommodation: One or two pilots on flight deck. Provision for four passengers
Armament and equipment: Four underwing hardpoints, each capable of carrying 350 lb (159 kg). Stores can include SUU-11A/A 7.62 mm gun pods; FFV UNI 12.75 mm gun pods; LAU-32A/A, 32B/A, 59A, 68A and 68B/A rocket launchers; CBU-14 and SUU-14/A bomb containers; LUU-1B, 5B and Mod 6 Mk 3 markers; Mk 24 flares; ADSID air-delivered seismic detection sensors; and a combined search radar and speaker system
In service with: Air forces of Haiti, Honduras, Nicaragua and Senegal; Royal Thai Navy

First flight about 1954

TUPOLEV Tu-16 (USSR) and XIAN B-6 (China)

NATO Reporting Name *Badger*
Medium bomber, reconnaissance-bomber and ECM aircraft
Photo: Tu-16 *(Badger-G)*, carrying two *Kingfish* missiles
Drawing: Tu-16 *(Badger-F)*, with additional side view (bottom) of
Badger-D **Data:** Tu-16 *(Badger-A)*

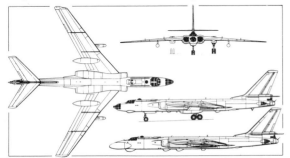

Power plant: Two Mikulin AM-3 turbojet engines (each 19 285 lb;
8 750 kg st)
Wing span: 108 ft 0½ in (32.93 m)
Length overall: 114 ft 2 in (34.80 m)
Normal T-O weight: 158 730 lb (72 000 kg)
Max level speed: 535 knots (616 mph; 992 km/h)
Service ceiling: 40 350 ft (12 300 m)
Range with max bomb load: 2 605 nm (3 000 miles; 4 800 km)
Range with max fuel: 3 110 nm (3 579 miles; 5 760 km)
Accommodation: Crew of six

Armament: Seven 23 mm guns: in twin-gun turrets above front
fuselage, under rear fuselage, and in tail, with single gun on starboard side of nose. Up to 19 800 lb (9 000 kg) of nuclear and
conventional bombs in internal weapons bay
Variants:
Badger-A: Basic strategic bomber, described above. Glazed nose.
Radar under fuselage in line with flight deck. Some now equipped
as flight refuelling tankers
Badger-C: Anti-shipping version, with *Kipper* winged missile carried under fuselage. Wide nose radome, in place of glazing and
nose gun of *Badger-A*.
Badger-D: Maritime/electronic reconnaissance version, with nose
like that of *Badger-C*. Larger undernose radome. Three blister fair-
ings in tandem under centre-fuselage
Badger-E: Similar to *Badger-A* but with cameras in weapons bay
Badger-F: Similar to *Badger-E* but with electronic intelligence pod
on pylon under each wing
Badger-G: Similar to *Badger-A* but with underwing pylons to carry
two rocket-powered air-to-surface missiles (NATO *Kelt*). Has been
seen also with new *Kingfish* missile on each pylon
Badger-H: Stand-off or escort ECM aircraft, with primary function
of chaff-dispensing
Badger-J: Specialised ECM jamming aircraft. Some equipment in
canoe-shape radome inside weapons bay
Badger-K: Electronic reconnaissance variant. Radomes inside and
forward of weapons bay
Xian B-6: Western designation for Chinese-built version of
Badger-A; Chinese designation is *H-6*
In service with: Air forces of China (B-6), Egypt *(Badger-G)*, Iraq
(Badger-A) and USSR (Air Force and Navy)

233

NATO Reporting Name *Blinder*
Three-seat supersonic bomber

Photo: Tu-22 *(Blinder-C)*
Drawing: Tu-22 *(Blinder-A)*, with scrap view of *Blinder-D*
Data: *Blinder-A,* estimated

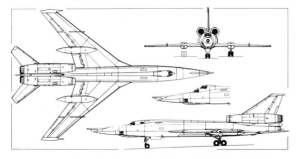

Power plant: Two turbojet engines (each 27 000 lb; 12 250 kg st with afterburning)
Wing span: 90 ft 10½ in (27.70 m)

Length overall: 132 ft 11½ in (40.53 m)
Max T-O weight: 184 970 lb (83 900 kg)
Max level speed at 40 000 ft (12 200 m): Mach 1.4 (800 knots; 920 mph; 1 480 km/h)
Service ceiling: 60 000 ft (18 300 m)
Max range: 1 215 nm (1 400 miles; 2 250 km)
Accommodation: Crew of three, in tandem
Armament: Weapons bay for free-fall nuclear and conventional bombs. Single 23 mm gun in radar-directed tail mounting
Variants:
Blinder-A: Basic medium-range reconnaissance bomber, described above
Blinder-B: Similar to *Blinder-A* but able to carry an air-to-surface missile (NATO *Kitchen*) with a 460 mile (740 km) range, recessed into the weapon bay. Larger radar and partially-retractable flight refuelling probe in nose
Blinder-C: Maritime reconnaissance version, with windows for six cameras in weapons bay doors. New dielectric panels, modifications to nosecone, etc on some aircraft suggest added equipment for ECM and electronic intelligence roles
Blinder-D: Training version. Cockpit for instructor in raised position aft of normal flight deck, with stepped-up canopy
In service with: Air forces of Iraq *(Blinder-A)* and Libya *(Blinder-B)*, Soviet Air Force and Navy

First flight about 1969

TUPOLEV Tu-22M/Tu-26* (USSR)

NATO Reporting Name *Backfire*
Long-range variable-geometry supersonic bomber

Photo, Drawing and Data: *Backfire-B*

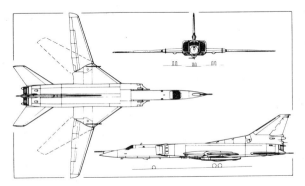

Power plant: Two turbofan engines (possibly Kuznetsov NK-144s, each more than 44 090 lb; 20 000 kg st with afterburning)
Wing span: spread: 113 ft (34.45 m); swept: 86 ft (26.21 m)
Length overall: 132 ft (40.23 m)
Max T-O weight: approx 270 000 lb (122 500 kg)
Armament: Twin 23 mm guns in radar-directed tail mounting.

Nominal weapon load 20,800 lb (9 435 kg). Primary armament of one *Kitchen* air-to-surface missile semi-recessed in underside of centre-fuselage. *Backfire* can also carry the full range of Soviet free-fall nuclear and conventional weapons, and a Naval aircraft photographed by the Swedish Air Force in 1978 had multiple racks for external stores under the front of its air intake trunks. Soviet development of decoy missiles has been reported, to supplement very advanced ECM and ECCM
Max level speed: Mach 2 (1 150 knots; 1 320 mph; 2 125 km/h) at high altitude; Mach 0.9 (595 knots; 685 mph; 1 100 km/h) at low altitude
Max unrefuelled combat range: 4 350 nm (5 000 miles; 8 050 km)
Variants:
Backfire-A: Initial version, with main undercarriage units retracting into typical Tupolev pods on wing trailing-edges. Because of disappointing range, only sufficient aircraft for one squadron built
Backfire-B: Main production version for Soviet Air Force and Navy. Wing span increased. Undercarriage pods reduced to small underwing fairings. Dismountable flight refuelling probe on nose. About 150 operational in early 1981, with deliveries continuing at rate of at least 30 a year, divided equally between the Soviet strategic bomber force and Naval Air Force
In service with: Soviet Air Force and Navy

*In public statements and documents, Western defence agencies seem prepared to adopt the designation Tu-22M by which Soviet delegates to the SALT II discussions referred to this aircraft. It might be premature to forget that the US Department of Defense used Tu-26 in earlier references to *Backfire*

First flight about 1961

TUPOLEV Tu-28P* (USSR)

NATO Reporting Name *Fiddler*
Tandem two-seat all-weather interceptor

Data: estimated

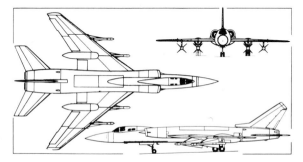

Power plant: Two afterburning turbojet engines (each 27 000 lb;
12 250 kg st)
Wing span: 65 ft 0 in (20.00 m)
Length overall: 85 ft 0 in (26.00 m)
Max T-O weight: 100 000 lb (45 000 kg)
Max level speed at 36 000 ft (11 000 m): Mach 1.75 (1 000 knots;
1 150 mph; 1 850 km/h)
Service ceiling: 65 620 ft (20 000 m)
Range: 2 700 nm (3 100 miles; 5 000 km)
Armament: Four missiles (NATO *Ash*), two under each wing—one
usually of the radar homing type and the other of the infra-red
homing type
In service with: Soviet Air Force

*Sometimes referred to as Tu-128 by US Department of Defense

NATO Reporting Name *Bear*
Long-range bomber (Tu-95) and maritime reconnaissance aircraft
(Tu-142)
Photo: Tu-95 *(Bear-B)* with *Kangaroo* missile
Drawing: Tu-142 *(Bear-D)*
Data: Tu-95 *(Bear-A)*

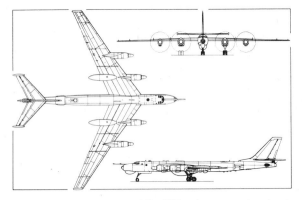

Power plant: Four Kuznetsov NK-12MV turboprop engines (each
14 795 ehp)
Wing span: approx 159 ft 0 in (48.50 m)

Length overall: approx 155 ft 10 in (47.50 m)
Max T-O weight: approx 340 000 lb (154 220 kg)
Max level speed at 41 000 ft (12 500 m): 434 knots (500 mph; 805
km/h)
Range with max bomb load: 6 775 nm (7 800 miles; 12 555 km)
Armament: Three pairs of 23 mm cannon in remotely-controlled
dorsal and ventral barbettes and tail position. Up to 25 000 lb
(11 340 kg) of bombs in internal weapons bay
Variants:
Bear-A: Long-range strategic bomber, described above
Bear-B: As *Bear-A* but equipped to carry large air-to-surface missile
(NATO *Kangaroo*) under fuselage, with associated radar in large
undernose radome, replacing glazed nose. A few, fitted with large
flight refuelling nose-probe, are used for maritime patrol. Others
are equipped to carry *Kitchen* air-to-surface missiles
Bear-C: Differs from *Bear-B* in having a streamlined blister fairing
on the port side of its rear fuselage as well as on the starboard side
Bear-D: Version with X-band radar in large blister fairing under
centre-fuselage, for reconnaissance and for pinpointing of targets
for missile launch crews on board ships and other aircraft. Glazed
nose like *Bear-A,* with undernose radome and superimposed
refuelling probe. Rear fuselage blisters as on *Bear-C.* Added fairings at tips of tailplane. One has been photographed with a faired
tail housing special equipment, in place of normal turret and
radome
Bear-E: Maritime reconnaissance bomber. As *Bear-A* but with rear
fuselage blister fairings and refuelling probe as on *Bear-C.* Six or
seven camera windows in weapons bay doors

(cont on page 243)

NATO Reporting Name *Moss*
Airborne warning and control aircraft

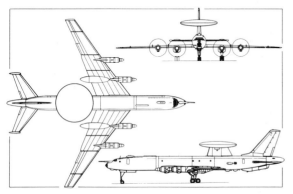

Power plant: Four Kuznetsov NK-12MV turboprop engines (each 14 795 ehp)
Wing span: 168 ft 0 in (51.20 m)
Length overall: 181 ft 1 in (55.20 m)
Max T-O weight: 374 785 lb (170 000 kg)
Max level speed: 459 knots (528 mph; 850 km/h)
Normal operating speed: 351 knots (404 mph; 650 km/h)
Max range without flight refuelling: 6 775 nm (7 800 miles; 12 550 km)
Accommodation: Basic crew of twelve
Armament and equipment: No guns. Early warning radar, in 36 ft (11 m) diameter rotating 'saucer' above fuselage, is said to operate effectively only over water
In service with: Soviet Air Force

Tupolev Tu-95/Tu-142 *(cont from page 241)*

Bear-F: Maritime version. Smaller X-band radar fairing, further forward than that of *Bear-D*. No blister fairings on rear fuselage. Lengthened nose, with shallow undernose radome on some aircraft only. Enlarged fairings aft of inboard engine nacelles to improve aerodynamics. Armament reduced to two guns, in tail mounting. Two stores bays in rear fuselage, one replacing ventral gun turret. Span 167 ft 8 in (51.10 m); length 162 ft 5 in (49.50 m), max T-O weight 414 470 lb (188 000 kg)
In service with: Soviet Air Force (Tu-95) and Navy (Tu-142)

Single-seat carrier- and land-based attack aircraft, and two-seat operational trainer
Photo: A-7E Corsair II
Drawing and Data: A-7D Corsair II

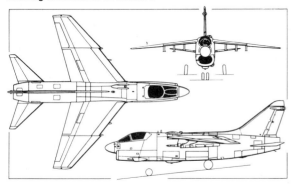

Power plant: One Allison TF41-A-1 (Rolls-Royce Spey 168-62) non-afterburning turbofan engine (14 250 lb; 6 465 kg st)
Wing span: 38 ft 9 in (11.80 m)
Length overall: 46 ft 1½ in (14.06 m)
Max T-O weight: 42 000 lb (19 050 kg)
Max level speed at S/L: 606 knots (698 mph; 1 123 km/h)
Max ferry range: with max internal and external fuel: 2 494 nm (2 871 miles; 4 621 km)
Armament: One M61A1 Vulcan 20 mm multi-barrel cannon in fuselage; two stations under fuselage and six under wings for more than 15 000 lb (6 805 kg) of external stores including air-to-air missiles, air-to-surface missiles, bombs, rockets and gun pods
Variants:
A-7A: Initial USN attack version; Pratt & Whitney TF30-P-6 turbofan engine (11 350 lb; 5 150 kg st)
A-7B: Developed A-7A; TF30-P-8 engine (12 200 lb; 5 534 kg st
A-7C: Designation of first 67 A-7Es, which had TF30-P-8 engines
TA-7C: Tandem two-seat operational trainer; converted from A-7B and A-7C. TF30-P-408 engine (13 400 lb; 6 078 kg st). Nav/weapons delivery systems as for A-7E
A-7D: USAF tactical fighter; TF41 turbofan standard (see data); navigation/weapon delivery system includes capability for all-weather radar bomb delivery. All being passed to Air National Guard
A-7E: USN attack/close support/interdiction version, similar to A-7D. First 67 re-designated A-7C; remainder have TF41-A-2 engine (15 000 lb; 6 800 kg st) as standard. Late-production models have a 720 lb (327 kg) FLIR (forward-looking infra-red) pod under starboard wing to improve night capability. Other A-7Es are being retrofitted with FLIR
A-7H: Land-based A-7E for Greece; folding wings retained
TA-7H: Two-seat operational trainer for Greece, with TF41-A-400 engine. As TA-7C but without flight refuelling capability
A-7K: Two-seat operational training version of A-7D for Air National Guard. Combat capability retained
A-7P: Refurbished A-7As for Portuguese Air Force, with TF30-P-408 engine and A-7E-standard avionics
In service with: Air forces of Greece (A-7H and TA-7H), Portugal (A-7P) and USA (Air Force, A-7D and A-7K; Navy, A-7A, A-7B, A-7C, TA-7C, A-7E)

Single-seat carrier-based limited all-weather fighter (F-8) and reconnaissance aircraft (RF-8)

Photo: F-8H Crusader
Drawing and Data: F-8E Crusader

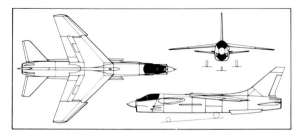

Power plant: One Pratt & Whitney J57-P-20 turbojet engine (18 000 lb; 8 165 kg st with afterburning)

Wing span: 35 ft 8 in (10.87 m)
Length overall: 54 ft 6 in (16.61 m)
Max T-O weight: 34 000 lb (15 420 kg)
Max level speed: nearly 1 148 knots (1 322 mph; 2 127 km/h)
Service ceiling: 58 000 ft (17 680 m)
Combat radius: 521 nm (600 miles; 965 km)
Armament: Four 20 mm Colt cannon in nose. Four Sidewinder missiles on sides of fuselage. Late-production F-8Es have two underwing pylons for weapons including two 1 000 lb or 2 000 lb bombs, four 500 lb bombs, twelve 250 lb bombs or 24 Zuni rockets. Eight more Zunis can replace the Sidewinders
Current variants:
F-8E (FN): Export fighter for French Navy; provision for Matra R530 missiles in addition to Sidewinders; blown flaps
RF-8G: Modernisation of RF-8A reconnaissance version with updated equipment. Cameras in lower front fuselage. Pratt & Whitney J57-P-4A turbojet engine (16 200 lb; 7 327 kg st)
F-8H: Modernised version of F-8D single-seat fighter, with updated equipment and attack capability. J57-P-20 engine
In service with: Navies of France (F-8E (FN)) and USA (RF-8G), Air Force of the Philippines (F-8H)

First flight 1969

Multi-purpose helicopter
Photo: Sea King HAS Mk 5
Drawing: Sea King HAS Mk 2
Data: Sea King Mk 50

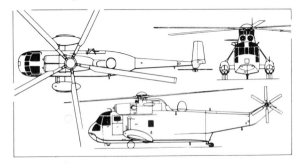

Power plant: Two Rolls-Royce Gnome H.1400-1 turboshaft engines (each 1 660 shp)
Main rotor diameter: 62 ft 0 in (18.90 m)
Length of fuselage: 55 ft 9¾ in (17.01 m)
Max T-O weight: 21 000 lb (9 525 kg)
Cruising speed at S/L: 112 knots (129 mph; 208 km/h)
Max rate of climb at S/L: 2 020 ft (616 m)/min
Service ceiling, one engine out: 4 000 ft (1 220 m)
Range with max standard fuel: 664 nm (764 miles; 1 230 km)
Operational equipment, ASW model: Plessey Type 195 dipping
sonar, AD 580 Doppler navigation system, AW 391 search radar in dorsal radome, transponder beneath rear fuselage, two No 4 marine markers, four No 2 Mk 2 smoke floats, up to four Mk 46 homing torpedoes or four Mk 11 depth charges or one Clevite simulator. For secondary roles a mounting for a machine-gun is provided on the aft frame of the starboard door
Current variants:
Mk 41, 43, 48: Search and rescue versions of original Royal Navy HAS Mk 1 for Germany, Norway and Belgium respectively, with 1 500 shp Gnome H.1400 engines and five-blade tail rotor
Mk 42, 45, 47: ASW versions of HAS Mk 1 for India, Pakistan and Egypt respectively
Mk 50: Improved multi-role version for Australia; uprated engines (see data), six-blade tail rotor, increased AUW and other detail improvements
HAS Mk 2: Similar to Mk 50, for ASW and SAR duties with Royal Navy. HAS Mk 1s were updated to Mk 2 standard. Mk 2s now being upgraded to Mk 5 standard
HAR Mk 3: Similar to Mk 50, for search and rescue duties with RAF
HC Mk 4: Utility version of Westland Commando Mk 2 for Royal Navy, with non-retractable landing gear
HAS Mk 5: Latest ASW and SAR version for Royal Navy, able to pinpoint enemy submarines at far greater range. Marconi LAPADS (lightweight acoustic processing and display system) passive sonobuoy processor, able to monitor signals from RAF Nimrod aircraft in joint search. MEL Sea Searcher radar in enlarged dorsal radome, etc
In service with: Air forces of Belgium and Norway, and Navies of Australia, Egypt, German Federal Republic, India, Pakistan and UK (Navy, HAS Mks 2 and 5 and HC Mk 4; Air Force HAR Mk 3)

Light liaison (Scout) or anti-submarine helicopter (Wasp)

Photo: Scout AH Mk 1
Drawing and Data: Wasp HAS Mk 1

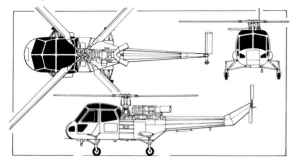

Power plant: One Rolls-Royce Nimbus 503 turboshaft engine (derated to 710 shp)

Main rotor diameter: 32 ft 3 in (9.83 m)
Length overall, rotors turning: 40 ft 4 in (12.29 m)
Max T-O weight: 5 500 lb (2 495 kg)
Max level speed at S/L: 104 knots (120 mph; 193 km/h)
Max rate of climb at S/L: 1 440 ft (439 m)/min
Max range with standard fuel: 263 nm (303 miles; 488 km)
Range with max fuel: including allowances of 5 min for T-O and landing, and 15 min cruising at best cruising height, with 4 passengers: 234 nm (270 miles; 435 km)
Armament: Two Mk 44 homing torpedoes or other stores carried externally
Variants:
Scout AH Mk 1: British Army 5-seat general-purpose version; Nimbus 101 or 102 engine (685 shp), full tailplane below boom, tubular skid landing gear. Export version similar
Wasp HAS Mk 1: Royal Navy ASW version, as described. Castoring 4-wheel landing gear, folding tail section with half-tailplane at top of fin on starboard side. Export versions similar
In service with: *Scout:* Bahrain Police and British Army (AH Mk 1). *Wasp:* Navies of Brazil, Netherlands, New Zealand, South Africa and UK (HAS Mk 1)

WESTLAND WESSEX (UK) and SIKORSKY S-58/H-34 SEABAT, SEAHORSE and CHOCTAW (USA)

Anti-submarine and general-purpose helicopter

Photo and Data: Wessex HU Mk 5
Drawing: Wessex HC Mk 2

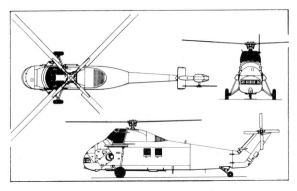

Power plant: One Rolls-Royce Gnome Mk 112 and one Gnome Mk 113 turboshaft engines (each 1 350 shp) coupled to give max 1 550 shp at rotor head
Main rotor diameter: 56 ft 0 in (17.07 m)
Length overall: 65 ft 9 in (20.03 m)

Max T-O weight: 13 500 lb (6 120 kg)
Max level speed at S/L: 115 knots (132 mph; 212 km/h)
Max rate of climb at S/L: 1 650 ft (503 m)/min
Service ceiling: 14 100 ft (4 300 m)
Range with max fuel: 415 nm (478 miles; 770 km)
Accommodation: Crew of one to three. Either 16 passengers, seven stretchers or 4 000 lb (1 814 kg) of freight
Armament: Provision for carrying anti-tank missiles or other air-to-surface weapons
Variants still in service:
Wessex HC Mk 2: RAF utility transport, generally similar to HU Mk 5 but with Gnome Mk 110/111 engines. Mk 52 similar
Wessex HAS Mk 3: RN anti-submarine and assault version. One 1 600 shp Napier Gazelle Mk 165 turboshaft. Dorsal radome. Armed normally with two homing torpedoes, replaceable with four SS.11 wire-guided missiles, machine-guns or 2 in rockets. Mk 31 similar except for 1 540 shp Gazelle 162 engine
Wessex HCC Mk 4: Two converted Mk 2s for The Queen's Flight
Wessex HU Mk 5: For Commando assault duties from RN carriers
CH-34A/C Choctaw: Utility/flying crane version, with 1 525 hp Wright R-1820-84 piston engine. Crew of two, 18 passengers or eight stretchers
UH-34D Seahorse: Utility transport
SH-34J Seabat: Anti-submarine version
In service with: *Wessex:* Royal Australian Navy (HAS Mk 31), Iraq (Mk 52), RAF (Mk 2 and 4), RN (Mk 3 and 5). *S-58:* Central African Republic, Costa Rica, France, Haiti, Indonesia (UH-34D), Nicaragua (CH-34A), Philippines (UH-34), Taiwan (CH-34), Thailand (CH-34C), US Army (CH-34) and Uruguayan Navy (SH-34J)

First flight 1971

WESTLAND/AÉROSPATIALE LYNX (UK/France)

General-purpose and anti-submarine helicopter
Photo: Lynx AH Mk 1 firing a TOW anti-tank missile
Drawing: Lynx HAS Mk 2
Data: Lynx Mk 80 series ASW version

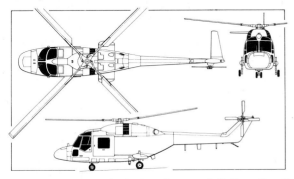

Power plant: Early production Lynx have two Rolls-Royce Gem 2 turboshaft engines (each 900 shp max contingency rating). Current models in Mk 80 series have Gem 41-1 engines (each 1 120 shp max contingency rating)
Main rotor diameter: 42 ft 0 in (12.80 m)
Length overall, rotors turning: 49 ft 9 in (15.16 m)
Max T-O weight: 10 500 lb (4 763 kg)
Max continuous cruising speed at S/L: 125 knots (144 mph; 232 km/h)

Max rate of climb at S/L: 2 170 ft (661 m)/min
Typical radius at S/L with crew of 3: search and rescue, 2 survivors: 115 nm (132 miles; 213 km)
Max range: 320 nm (368 miles; 593 km)
Armament, ASW mission: Two Mk 44 or Mk 46 homing torpedoes or two Mk 11 depth charges, mounted externally one each side of the cabin. Sea Skua semi-active homing missiles for attacking light surface craft; alternatively, four AS.12 or similar wire-guided missiles. Equipment can include dipping sonar or MAD
Variants:
AH Mk 1: British Army general-purpose/utility version. Tubular skid landing gear. Cabin space for pilot and up to 10 troops, 2 000 lb (907 kg) of freight, or 3 stretchers and attendant. Provision for armament, rescue hoist, external cargo hook etc, according to mission
HAS Mk 2: Royal Navy shipborne version, for ASW and other duties. Seaspray radar in shorter, blunter nose; castoring tricycle landing gear; folding tail section
Mk 2 French Navy version: Generally similar to HAS Mk 2 but with more advanced target detection gear
Mk 21: For ASW, SAR and other duties with Brazilian Navy
Mk 23: For ASW duties with Argentinian Navy
Mk 25 (SH-14B): For ASW duties with Royal Netherlands Navy
Mk 27 (UH-14A): SAR, communications and training version for Royal Netherlands Navy
Mk 28: General-purpose military version for Qatar
Mk 80: For coastal surveillance and fishery protection duties with Danish Navy. First of new series with uprated Gem 41-1 engines and increased AUW

(cont on page 257)

YAKOVLEV Yak-28 and Yak-28P (USSR)

NATO Reporting Names *Firebar, Brewer* and *Maestro*
Two-seat multi-purpose tactical aircraft (Yak-28 *Brewer*), all-weather fighter (Yak-28P *Firebar*) and operational trainer *(Maestro)*

Photo: *Brewer*
Drawing and estimated Data: Yak-28P *(Firebar)*

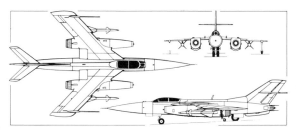

Power plant: Two turbojet engines, believed to be of same basic type as Tumansky R-11 fitted to some MiG-21s (each 13 120 lb; 5 950 kg st with afterburning)

Wing span: 42 ft 6 in (12.95 m)
Length overall: 71 ft 0½ in (21.65 m)
Max T-O weight: 35 000 lb (15 875 kg)
Max level speed at 35 000 ft (10 670 m): Mach 1.1 (636 knots; 733 mph; 1 180 km/h)
Service ceiling: 55 000 ft (16 750 m)
Max range: 1 040-1 390 nm (1 200-1 600 miles; 1 930-2 575 km)
Armament: Pylon under each outer wing for *Anab* air-to-air missile, with alternative infra-red or semi-active radar homing heads
Variants:
Brewer-A/B/C: Two-seat tactical attack versions, with navigator/bomb aimer in glazed nose. Most have radome under forward fuselage. One or two guns in sides of fuselage. Internal bomb bay. Can have long or short engine nacelles
Brewer-D: Similar to *Brewer-A/B/C*, but reconnaissance cameras in bomb-bay
Brewer-E: Active ECM pack in bomb bay, from which it projects. Rocket pod under each outer wing
Firebar: Tandem two-seat all-weather fighter, described above. Radar in 'solid' nose. Long nacelles
Maestro: Trainer version of *Firebar*. Two cockpits in tandem, with individual canopies
In service with: Soviet Air Force

Westland/Aérospatiale Lynx *(cont from page 255)*

Mk 81 (SH-14C): Uprated ASW version for Royal Netherlands Navy
Mk 86: Uprated version for coastguard, fishery and oil rig protection duties with Royal Norwegian Air Force

Mk 88: Uprated ASW and anti-shipping version for Federal German Navy
In service with: Armed forces of Argentina, Brazil, Denmark, France, German Federal Republic, Netherlands, Norway, Qatar and UK

First flight probably early 1970s

NATO Reporting Name *Forger*
Single-seat VTOL carrier-based combat aircraft and two-seat trainer

Photo, Drawing and Data: *Forger-A*

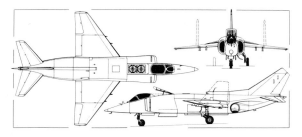

Power plant: One unidentified turbojet engine, without afterburner, based possibly on Lyulka AL-21 (17 500 lb; 7 940 kg st) as primary power plant, exhausting through two vectored-thrust nozzles, one each side of rear fuselage. Two Koliesov lift-jet engines (each 5 600-8 000 lb; 2 540-3 625 kg st) mounted in tandem aft of cockpit, in such a way that their thrust is exerted upward and slightly forward. Main vectored-thrust nozzles turn about 10° forward of vertical during take-off and landing; but Yak-36MP does not appear to possess capability of STOL take-off, or thrust vectoring in forward flight to increase manoeuvrability (techniques employed as routine with Harrier)

Wing span: 23 ft 0 in (7.00 m)
Length overall: 49 ft 3 in (15.00 m)
Max T-O weight: 22 050 lb (10 000 kg)
Max level speed at 36 000 ft (11 000 m): Mach 1.3 (745 knots; 860 mph; 1 380 km/h)
Max rate of climb at S/L: 14 750 ft (4 500 m)/min
Service ceiling: 39 375 ft (12 000 m)
Armament: Four underwing pylons for air-to-air missiles, gun pods, rocket packs and other stores
Variants:
Forger-A: Basic single-seat attack/reconnaissance aircraft. At least nine carried by each Soviet carrier/cruiser of *Kiev* class
Forger-B: Two-seat trainer. Second cockpit forward of normal cockpit, at lower level, with single, continuous blister canopy, giving considerable nose droop. Rear fuselage lengthened to compensate for longer nose. No ranging radar or weapon pylons. Overall length about 58 ft (17.66 m)
In service with: Soviet Navy, on board carrier *Kiev* and sister ships

INDEX

A

A-4 Skyhawk, McDonnell Douglas 155
A-5, Nanchang 189
A-6 Intruder, Grumman 93
A-7 Corsair, Vought 245
A-10A Thunderbolt II, Fairchild Republic 81
A-37 Dragonfly, Cessna 53
AEW Nimrod Mk 3, BAe 27
AH-1 Hueycobra & Seacobra, Bell 31
AH-64, Hughes 119
AV-8B Advanced Harrier, McDonnell Douglas 21
Advanced Harrier, McDonnell Douglas AV-8B 21
Aeritalia G91 7
Aermacchi:
 MB 326 9
 MB 339K Veltro 11
Aérospatiale Super Frelon 13
Aérospatiale/Westland:
 Lynx 255
 Puma 15
Ajeet, HAL 105
Alize, Breguet 45
Alpha Jet, Dassault-Breguet/Dornier 73
Argus, Canadair CP-107 51
Atlantic, Breguet 47
Aurora, Lockheed CP-104 141
(Avro) Shackleton, Hawker Siddeley 115

B

B-2 Super Mystère, Dassault 71
B-5, Harbin 127
B-6, Xian (Tupolev) 233
B-52 Stratofortress, Boeing 37
B-57, Martin 149

BAC 167 Strikemaster, BAe 29
Be-12 *Mail*, Beriev 35
BO 105, MBB 151
BAC Lightning 17
BAe:
 Harrier 19
 Sea Harrier 21
 Hawk 23
 Nimrod MR Mk 1 & 2 25
 Nimrod AEW Mk 3 27
 Jet Provost 29
 Strikemaster (BAC 167) 29
Bell:
 AH-1 Hueycobra & Seacobra 31
 Model 206L TexasRanger 33
Beriev *Mail* (Be-12) 35
Boeing:
 B-52 Stratofortress 37
 E-3A Sentry 39
 E-4 41
 EC-135 43
 KC-135 Stratotanker 43
 RC-135 43
Breguet:
 Alizé 45
 Atlantic 47
Bronco, Rockwell OV-10 201
Buccaneer, Hawker Siddeley 113

C

CL-41/CT-114 Tutor, Canadair 49
CP-107 Argus, Canadair 51
CP-140 Aurora, Lockheed 141
Canadair:
 CL-41/CT-114 Tutor 49
 CP-107 Argus 51
Canberra, English Electric 79
Cessna:
 A-37 Dragonfly 53
 T-37 53
Choctaw, Sikorsky 253
Convair F-106 Delta Dart 55
Corsair, Vought A-7 245
Crusader, Vought F-8 247

D

Dassault:
 Étendard IV 57
 Mirage III 59
 Mirage IV-A 61
 Mirage 5 63
 Mirage 50 63
 Mirage F.1 65
 Mirage 2000 67
 Super Étendard 57
 Super Mirage 4000 69
 Super Mystere B-2 71
Dassault-Breguet/Dornier Alpha Jet 73
Defender, Hughes Model 500 121
de Havilland Venom 75
Delta Dart, Convair F-106 55
Dragonfly, Cessna A-37 53
Draken, Saab 35 203

E

E-2 Hawkeye, Grumman 97
E-3A Sentry, Boeing 39

E-4, Boeing 41
EA-6B Prowler, Grumman 95
EC-135, Boeing 43
EMB-III, Embraer 77
Eagle, McDonnell Douglas F-15 159
Eagle (Nesher) 123
Eagle (Orao/IAR-93), Soko/Cnair 219
Embraer EMB-III 77
English Electric Canberra 79
Étendard IV, Dassault 57
Extender, McDonnell Douglas KC-10A 163

F

F.1, Dassault Mirage 65
F-1, Mitsubishi 185
F-III, General Dynamics 89
F-4 Phantom II, McDonnell Douglas 157
F-5, Shenyang (Mikoyan) 169
F-5A+B, Northrop 197
F-5E, Northrop 197
F-5G, Northrop 197
F-6, Shenyang (Mikoyan) 167
F-7 Xian (Mikoyan) 169
F-14A Tomcat, Grumman 99
F-15 Eagle, McDonnell Douglas 159
F-16 Fighting Falcon, General Dynamics 87
F-86 Sabre, North American 191
F-100 Super Sabre, North American 193
F-101 Voodoo, McDonnell 153
F-104 Starfighter, Lockheed 137
F-105 Thunderchief, Fairchild Republic 83
F-106 Delta Dart, Convair 55
F/A-18 Hornet, McDonnell Douglas 161
FB-III, General Dynamics 191

Fairchild Republic:
  A-10A Thunderbolt II 95
  F-105 Thunderchief 83
Fighting Falcon, General Dynamics F-16 87
FMA IA 58 Pucara 85

G

G91, Aeritalia 57
General Dynamics:
  F-16 Fighting Falcon 87
  F-III 89
  FB-III 91
Gnat, Hawker Siddeley/HAL 105
Grumman:
  A-6 Intruder 93
  EA-6B Prowler 95
  E-2 Hawkeye 97
  F-14A Tomcat 99
  OV-1 Mohawk 101
  S-2 Tracker 103

H

H-3 Sea King, Sikorsky 213
HF-24 Marut, HAL 107
HS Nimrod MR Mks 1+2, BAe 25
HS Nimrod AEW Mk 3, BAe 27
HAL:
  Ajeet 105
  HF-24 Marut 107
Handley Page Victor 109
Harbin B-5 127
Harrier, BAe 19
Hawk, BAe 23

Hawker Hunter 111
Hawker Siddeley:
  (Avro) Shackleton 115
  Buccaneer 113
  Vulcan 117
Hawker Siddeley/HAL Gnat 105
Hawkeye, Grumman E-2 97
Hornet, McDonnell Douglas F/A-18 161
Hueycobra, Bell AH-1 31
Hughes:
  AH-64 119
  Model 500 MD Defender 121
Hunter, Hawker 111

I

IAI Kfir (Lion Cub) 123
Ilyushin:
  Il-18 125
  Il-28 127
  Il-38 129

J

J-1 Jastreb, Soko 217
Jaguar, Sepecat 209
Jastreb, Soko J-1 217
Jet Provost, BAe 29

K

Ka-25, Kamov 133
KC-10A Extender, McDonnell Douglas 163
KC-135 Stratotanker, Boeing 43

Kaman SH-2F Seasprite
Kamov Ka-25
Kawasaki P-2J

L

Lightning, BAC
Lockheed:
  CP-140 Aurora
  F-104 Starfighter
  P-2 Neptune
  P-3 Orion
  S-3A Viking
  SR-71A
  TR-1
  U-2
Lynx, Westland/Aérospatiale

M

M-4, Myasishchev
Mail, Beriev Be-12
MB 326, Aermacchi
MB 339K Veltro 2, Aermacchi
Mi-8, Mil
Mi-14, Mil
Mi-24, Mil
Mi-24, Mil
MiG-17, Mikoyan/Gurevich
MiG-19, Mikoyan
MiG-21, Mikoyan
MiG-23, Mikoyan
MiG-25, Mikoyan

131	MiG-27, Mikoyan
133	Martin B-57
135	Marut, HAL HF-24
	MBB BO 105
	McDonnell F-101 Voodoo
	McDonnell Douglas:
17	A-4 Skyhawk
21	AV-8B Advanced Harrier
157	F-4 Phantom II
159	F-15 Eagle
161	F/A-18 Hornet
163	KC-10A Extender
	Mikoyan/Gurevich:
165	MiG-17
167	MiG-19
169	MiG-21
171	MiG-23
173	MiG-25
175	MiG-27
	Mil:
	Mi-8
177	Mi-14
179	Mi-24
181	Mi-24
183	Mirage III, Dassault
59	Mirage IV-A, Dassault
61	Mirage 5, Dassault
63	Mirage 50, Dassault
63	Mirage F.1, Dassault
65	Mirage 2000, Dassault
67	Mitsubishi F-1
185	Model 206L TexasRanger, Bell
33	Model 500 MD Defender, Hughes
121	Mohawk, Grumman OV-1
101	Myasishchev M-4

175		**N**
149	Nanchang A-5	189
107	Neptune, Lockheed P-2	139
151	Nesher (Eagle)	123
153	Nimrod MR Mks 1+2, BAe	25
	Nimrod AEW Mk 3, BAe	27
155	North American:	
	F-86 Sabre	191
157	F-100 Super Sabre	193
159	Northrop:	
161	F-5A+B	195
163	F-5E	197
	F-5G	197
165	Tiger II	197
167		
169		
171		
173		
175		**O**
	OV-1 Mohawk, Grumman	101
177	OV-10 Bronco, Rockwell	201
179	Orao/IAR-93, Soko/Cnair	219
181	Orion P-3, Lockheed	141
183		
59		
61		**P**
63	P-2 Neptune, Lockheed	139
63	P-2J, Kawasaki	135
65	P-3 Orion, Lockheed	141
67	PS-1, Shin Meiwa	211
185	Panavia Tornado	199
167	Phantom II, McDonnell Douglas F-4	157
169	Prowler, Grumman EA-6B	95
171	Pucara, FMA IA 58	85
173	Puma, Westland/Aérospatiale	15

R

RC-135, Boeing — 43
Rockwell OV-10 Bronco — 201

S

S-2 Tracker, Grumman — 103
S-3A Viking, Lockheed — 143
S-58/H-34 Seabat, Seahorse & Choctaw, Sikorsky — 253
S-61A/B, Sikorsky — 213
S-70L/SH-60B Seahawk, Sikorsky — 215
SH-2F Seasprite, Kaman — 131
SR-71A, Lockheed — 145
Su-7B, Sukhoi — 221
Su-9, Sukhoi — 223
Su-11, Sukhoi — 223
Su-15, Sukhoi — 225
Su-17, Sukhoi — 227
Su-20, Sukhoi — 227
Su-22, Sukhoi — 227
Su-24, Sukhoi — 229
Saab:
  Saab-35 Draken — 203
  Saab-37 Viggen — 205
  Saab-105 — 207
Sabre, North American F-86 — 191
Scout, Westland — 251
Seabat, Sikorsky S-58/H-34 — 253
Seacobra, Bell AH-1 — 31
Sea Harrier, BAe — 21
Seahawk, Sikorsky S-70L/SH-60B — 215
Seahorse, Sikorsky S-58/H34 — 253
Sea King, Sikorsky H-3 — 213
Sea King, Westland — 249
Seasprite, Kaman SH-2F — 131
Sentry, Boeing E-3A — 39
Sentry 02-337, Summit — 231
Sepecat, Jaguar — 209
Shackleton (Avro), Hawker Siddeley — 115
Shenyang F-5 — 165
Shenyang F-6 — 167
Shin Meiwa:
  PS-1 — 211
  US-1 — 211
Sikorsky:
  H-3 Sea King — 213
  S-58/H34 Seabat, Seahorse & Choctaw — 253
  S-61A/B — 213
  S-70L/SH-60B Seahawk — 215
Skyhawk, McDonnell Douglas A-4 — 155
Soko/Cnair Orao/IAR-93 — 219
Starfighter, Lockheed F-104 — 137
Stratofortress, Boeing B-52 — 37
Stratotanker, Boeing KC-135 — 43
Strikemaster (BAC 167), BAe — 29
Sukhoi:
  Su-7B — 221
  Su-9 — 223
  Su-11 — 223
  Su-15 — 225
  Su-17 — 227
  Su-20 — 227
  Su-22 — 229
  Su-24 — 229
Summit Sentry 02-337 — 231
Super Étendard, Dassault — 57
Super Frelon, Aérospatiale — 13
Super Mirage 4000, Dassault — 69
Super Mystère B-2, Dassault — 71
Super Sabre, North American F-100 — 193

T

T-37, Cessna — 53
TR-1, Lockheed — 147
Tu-16, Tupolev — 233
Tu-22, Tupolev — 235
Tu-22M/Tu-26, Tupolev — 237
Tu-28P/Tu-128, Tupolev — 239
Tu-95, Tupolev — 241
Tu-126, Tupolev — 243
Tu-142, Tupolev — 241
TexasRanger, Bell Model 206L — 33
Thunderbolt II, Fairchild Republic A-10A — 81
Thunderchief, Fairchild Republic F-105 — 83
Tiger II, Northrop — 197
Tomcat, Grumman F-14A — 99
Tornado, Panavia — 199
Tracker, Grumman S-2 — 103
Tupolev:
  Tu-16 — 233
  Tu-22 — 235
  Tu-22M/Tu-26 — 237
  Tu-28P/Tu-128 — 239
  Tu-95 — 241
  Tu-126 — 243
  Tu-142 — 241
Tutor, Canadair CL-41/CT-114 — 49

U

U-2, Lockheed — 147

V

Veltro 2, Aermacchi MB 339K 11
Venom, de Havilland 75
Victor, Handley Page 109
Viggen, Saab Saab-37 205
Viking, Lockheed S-3A 143
Voodoo, McDonnell F-101 153
Vought:
  A-7 Corsair 245
  F-8 Crusader 247
Vulcan, Hawker Siddeley 117

W

Wasp, Westland 251
Wessex, Westland 253
Westland: 249
  Sea King 251
  Scout 251
  Wasp 253
  Wessex 245
Westland/Aérospatiale: 247
  Puma 117
  Lynx 15

X

Xian B-6 233
Xian F-7 169

Y

Yakovlev:
  Yak-28 257
  Yak-28P 257
  Yak-36MP 259